1964

This book may be ke

BRINGING YOUR CHILD TO GOD

Bringing Your Child To God

The religious education of the pre-school child

Xavier Lefebvre SJ and
Louis Perin SJ

Translated by Marta Gondos

P. J. KENEDY & SONS — NEW YORK

Library of Congress Catalog Card No. 63-20401
NIHIL OBSTAT: ROBERTUS CANONICUS MEAGHER, CENSOR DEPUTATUS
IMPRIMATUR: T. ADAMSON, VIC. GEN.
LIVERPOLII, DIE 27 JUNII, 1963
Made and printed in Great Britain

CONTENTS

5

6 CONTENTS

8 CONTENTS

INTRODUCTION

WHEN THE time comes to begin a child's formal religious education many parents experience an embarrassment which increases in the years that follow. And even teachers in infant and elementary schools whose lot it is to teach religion to small children do not know how to set out a programme of religious education which is progressively adapted to these lower age groups.

To fill this need this book, basing its conclusions on a careful study of the psychological development of children, attempts to outline a programme of religious education for very young children.

There are many possible theories concerning the religious education of young children. Plenty of methods exist. Each has appreciable merits but to our knowledge there are few which are based both on direct observation of the children and on objective and detailed study of their psychology at each age.

Much research has been done in recent years in this field. At the same time, in the field of religious education we have come to realize that an astounding affinity exists between the soul of the child and such living sources of religion as the Bible and the Liturgy.

A reform of religious educational methods does seem inevitable, although it is as yet still in its infancy. This book attempts to make a contribution to the subject.

We have also thought it worth our while to make a study of a group of children who are living in a Christian environment. The majority of works written at present and the suggestions made in them try to solve the problems of children—unfortunately by far in the majority—who live in a de-Christianized milieu. Fortunately there still are children who live in a certain atmosphere of faith at home and have an opportunity to receive a Christian education at school.

We have spent nearly ten years studying children of this age, with the help of parents and teachers, in an attempt to come to know them better. We have sought to discover what their psychological needs and their human and spiritual resources are. Again with the help of their parents and teachers, we have pondered the implications of our findings for their education, and especially for their religious education.

Now a religious life, even though it has its essential source in the supernatural life received at Baptism, is grafted onto our human life and it is surely impossible to fill the spiritual needs of a child without first having an adequate idea of his human development.

This book, therefore, will consist of a first part giving a sketch of the pre-school child's psychology, with recommendations for his education in general; a second part dealing with his religious education in particular; and finally a third part with a suggested programme which follows closely the frame given by the liturgical year.

The principal aim of our work was not to set up a definite programme of religious education but rather to help educators achieve some co-ordination in the different spheres of a child's development—a co-ordination much to be desired, which can be especially helpful in unifying the education given by the family and the school.

If parents and teachers both draw inspiration from it, the same spirit will pervade the child's religious life at home and at school, the same programme will be followed by both. It will be possible for parents to make sure that religious instruction at school has been assimilated by their children and they can adapt family devotions to follow the programme.

Even those who do not follow to the letter the programme set out in this book will find here numerous practical suggestions as to how to keep the religious life of the child at home and at school in harmony with the liturgical year.

Some find it artificial that the programme is confined to children within definite age limits. Parents rarely notice such clear-cut development in their children, but teachers will not be of the same opinion : they know by experience that even though children taken individually develop each according to his own rhythm, yet when they are in groups, the average of all these individual developments obeys more definite laws. A class of three- and four-year-olds gives quite a different impression from a class of five-year-olds, and certain characteristics are invariably found in groups of children of a given age.

Nevertheless, educators will have to decide for themselves in the choice and application of the suggestions made here. Suggestions made for one age may sometimes be more suitably followed earlier or later and individual cases must always be taken into account. Parents and teachers must begin by observing the children in their charge, just as we have tried to do in the descriptions and programmes of our work.

We have purposely made no mention of a definite age in the title of this book. We have said 'pre-school children' because the traits peculiar to a given age often appear in the course of the year, and many children of five still resemble younger children in many respects.

May all those who encouraged us to take up this work and who helped us to complete it accept our sincere thanks.

May the years spent on this work bring some help to those who search gropingly for the best path to bring their children to God. This will be our best reward.

Sainte-Geneviève, Versailles.

PART ONE

THE CHARACTERISTICS OF THE YOUNG CHILD AND HIS EDUCATION

OUTLINE

IN ORDER to understand children of three and four years of age, it is necessary to realize that around the age of two or three the child makes an important discovery : he realizes that he has a will of his own, that he has the power to assert himself against the persons around him and to oppose them.

After the age of two—usually considered by mothers as a docile age, something of a golden age in infancy—the child's attitude frequently changes. Finding that he can resist those around him, he seems to be dominated by the need to oppose others in everything, with the sole purpose, it seems, of demonstrating his willpower. It is now that he starts to use the personal pronoun 'I' and not his own name when he talks, and the frequency with which he says 'I this . . .' 'I that . . .' expresses this desire to assert himself. When the crisis has passed (with or without storms), usually around three or three and a half, the child is no longer a baby tied to his mother's apron strings : he is a small 'grown-up' standing on his own two feet, with a dignity of his own, trying to assert himself and win respect from others.[1]

[1] N.B. We are speaking generally. It is not possible to give details of individual cases in a general description of the psychological stages which children generally go through. There are no absolute rules in this field. The descriptions of the different ages correspond to a mean established by observing large numbers of children and is true for the majority of cases studied. There

This change is first noticeable in the way the child looks at things and in the way his attitude to them has altered. We are dealing now with a real 'conqueror' valiantly trying to grasp everything around him, and at the same time a 'magician' who is becoming a little king in the universe which he creates for himself and who likes to assert himself unconditionally.

Fom now on the child needs to have around him people who appreciate his need to dominate and who take into account the magic quality of his thinking and his taste for the absolute. Especially when he is being introduced to religious things, the supernatural should be presented to him as faithfully as possible, that is, as something extraordinary, imposing, divine; but at the same time care should be taken that his imagination does not transform it into an unreal and fairy world.

This young 'conqueror-magician' needs a religion which is real and wonderful at the same time.

With this first step we have approached another aspect of the child's psychology which is of capital importance : his desire to grow. This is the social expression of his desire to assert himself. The child tries to raise himself to the level of those bigger than he is, especially the adults. He imitates them, he is sensitive to their opinion. To merit their good opinion and take part in the world of the 'grown-ups', he becomes capable, in spite of his taste for independence, of submitting to certain social constraints.

There is no greater motivating force for his education than this desire to grow and in his religious education we shall rely on it heavily : we shall introduce the child to a God of greatness, who wishes to see him grow and develop in every way; and we shall teach him how to do this.

A child who yearns to grow needs a religion which encourages growth.

is, however, no lack of exceptions. This holds for all generalizations which the reader will find in this book and it should be kept in mind.

Finally it will be seen that the desire to assert himself is accompanied in the depths of the child's consciousness by the need of a new love—a need which is unconditional and demanding, a source of jealousy and even anguish. Some children no longer find satisfaction in the emotional relationships which were satisfying enough for them before. Secretly they are yearning for a more personal, more exclusive love which sets them apart from others. The child himself is already capable of a love which is more personal and voluntary than it was before.

He needs to be given the security of a watchful and tranquil affection, and through his religion the child should know and feel himself loved by God, personally loved by him always, no matter what happens, and oriented towards an active love of God and others.

A child who yearns to be loved needs a religion which captivates his heart.

In this way, through an education and a religion which take into account these three essential needs—to assert himself, to grow and to be loved—the child of three to five years of age, instead of hardening in the egoism of his nascent personality, will begin to grow in charity before God.

1   THE CHILD NEEDS A RELIGION WHICH IS WONDERFUL AND WHICH IS REAL

THE SMALL child in his first months is entirely dependent on his surroundings and he is not conscious of being distinct from other beings. To the extent that he perceives them, he identifies himself with them. His senses serve him at first to adjust himself to his surroundings, and only later will they become the means to acquire knowledge. His eyes move when they see something move. The activity of his senses is merely unconscious imitation.

But soon his muscles start developing and through countless elementary experiences he learns that his body is something distinct and independent of external objects. From then on his life is dominated by two needs: the need to move and the need to experience. It gives him pleasure to try out his muscular strength; and it also gives him pleasure to see, to hear, to touch. His curiosity awakens.

At the age of three and four the child is still:

> *an impressionable being who is a reflection of the environment he lives in,*
> *an eager explorer who wants to take possession of the world around him;*
> *but now this little conqueror needs words in order to grasp things,*

*his imagination creates a special world of which he is the
    king,*
*his mind will accept as absolute truth every idea it en-
    counters.*

Let us look more closely at these psychological traits, each in
some way manifesting his need to assert himself, and see what
conclusions we should draw for his spiritual and temporal
education.

HE IS AN IMPRESSIONABLE BEING

WHO IS A REFLECTION OF

THE ENVIRONMENT HE LIVES IN

At the age of two the child is often already a faithful reflection of his environment: he accepts its controlling influence,
conforms to it, and lets himself be formed by it.[1] The child is
by then usually tidy, patient, amiable, kind, gay, or on the
contrary untidy, nervous, cross, and sad according to his
mother's mood. He cries if she cries and laughs if she laughs.

At the age of three and four, in spite of the fact that the
child's personality is beginning to emerge, his environment still
influences him strongly in many ways. It does so first of all
through influence and pressure, as it did in the earlier stages.
The child is naturally inclined to imitate what he sees done,
and if he is approached in the right way, he will often follow
suggestions made to him. But this imitativeness and conformity
take on a more personal character at this age.

For from now on his environment influences him more by
challenging him than by exerting pressure. Because the child
wants to assert himself, he tries to imitate those around him, in
order to have the joy of being equal to them, of feeling powerful, of playing at being 'somebody' by taking over other
people's personality.

Finally, it is by the reaction which it provokes from the
child that the environment has its deepest influence on him—
a reaction of acceptance or of rebellion, on which depend the

[1] Cf. note p. 15.

development or the repression of his personality. Let us give some examples.

If he is brought up by someone who is calm and orderly, not only will the child be inclined to imitate this, but as well he will experience a sense of security with this person and this will make him feel at peace. In the same way, with parents who are gentle yet firm the child will blossom out. If on the contrary he lives in contact with impatient adults who live in disorder, or with weak and vacillating parents, or cold and brutal teachers, the child will not only acquire something of their faults, but he will live in great uncertainty and dissatisfaction, and this will confuse him.

There are many ways out of this situation for him: to rebel or to let himself be passively led (or, more exactly, misled) by the contradictory orders of those around him—a situation which most often has the consequence of robbing him completely of initiative and naturalness; or he will seek unconsciously, under the appearance of normality, to satisfy his repressed nature by secret compensations: an excessively imaginative life, nightmares, manias, lies, thefts, greediness, etc. The education of a young child depends in the first place on the quality and character of his educators.

And we should make no mistake here: the child does not distinguish between the things purposely meant for his education and those not, and he is not formed only in the moments when we are occupied with him. It is at each and every moment that the child is being formed by what he sees and hears around him, often unnoticed by his educators. His parents and teachers will make a great mistake if they assume that their direct interventions into his life, that is, the orders they give and the behaviour they expressly impose on him, are the only things that count in his education. The child will develop in quite a different way, for example, according to whether he lives with embittered or with happy people. And, as a consequence, the atmosphere to which he is exposed in infancy will leave profound traces on his personality for the rest of his life.

THE IDEAL ATMOSPHERE FOR A GOOD EDUCATION

The first duty of parents and teachers is, therefore, to try to create an atmosphere around the child which will help him to develop.

What is this ideal atmosphere? The whole of this book will answer that question. However, at this stage we can already give some indication of the most important conditions necessary for the development of a Christian life.

A child of this age must first of all live surrounded by the *love* of his family, and must feel himself the object of a *personal* affection on the part of those educating him. A warm and comforting atmosphere is indispensable to his development. We shall speak of this point at length in the third part of this character sketch, when we are dealing with his emotional life.

From the age of three, this love must be accompanied by *respect* for a child who has begun to discover the independence of his will and who has now a personality of his own. Those around him should never forget that he is no longer the baby he was before, and that he must be spoken to and ordered about in a new way. The child feels that he is someone different from others, someone with a dignity of his own, and he is happy when treated with attention and respect. Thus treated, instead of remaining at the contradicting stage, he can become an agreeable companion and a self-confident and co-operative ally for the adult.

At the same time, it is just as necessary that the child submit to certain *requirements* : that is to say, fixed rules and habits, definite regulations and a discipline to which everyone submits. There is a fundamental reason for this which we shall discuss later when dealing with his instinctive sense of fairness and we shall explain there how a child can be led to obey. To achieve this requires authority and a just firmness, which do not in any way impede great love for the child nor the respect due to his liberty. Liberty is not the capricious and unbridled tyranny of a being abandoned to his instincts, any more than authority is the arbitrary tyranny of an adult who has no regard for the nature of the child.

The child also needs to have *calmness* around him, if possible habitual calmness : there should be no shouting, no arguments in front of him, no repeated loss of patience with him but, as far as possible, friendliness and evenness of humour. Our presence should radiate an amiable tranquillity, firm and self-confident. We know that this is to ask something difficult —'impossible', the majority of parents will say. But we cannot conceal that this condition is of capital importance for his equanimity and good education. All effort and progress in this direction, small as it may be, will be of great profit to the child. We should not discourage ourselves with the excuse that the ideal will never be achieved, but rather take up our task again each day and try to advance one step on this road, for the sake of our children.

In such an atmosphere the child can learn to be calm and self-controlled too. He should be shown how to do things properly : how to sit, open a door, carry something fragile, blow his nose, wash his hands . . .; if possible he should do some physical exercises daily, rhythmical marching, various movements, dances. . . .[1]

He should also learn how to be *silent*. At one time or another during the day, let us ask him to be silent for an instant, in a restful posture, so that he can hear far-away sounds. A small child loves to 'listen to the silence' in this way once he has been taught how. He is quite capable of it and finds satisfaction in the self-control which is needed for it. Montessori's 'lesson in silence' is most useful in this regard.

Let us try to instil in the child a sense of *respect* for the persons and things around him. He will acquire this naturally enough if he lives in an atmosphere of friendly politeness,

---

[1] Practical details on this subject will be found in our programme for the year (pp. 127-8). They are of interest mainly for the class teacher but can be useful for the parent too. The latter will find it useful to read the short but instructive booklet on self-control and silence (based on Montessori methods) : *L'education de l'homme conscient*, by Hélène Lubienska de Lenval (Spes, 1946).

where everyone and everything is treated with due consideration.[1]

And finally the child should feel himself surrounded by *joy*.
He is made for joy. It is then that he opens up to life and far
from being paralysed and under constraint, he spontaneously
makes use of all his potentialities.

A RELIGIOUS ATMOSPHERE

The same diverse qualities which are necessary for an educative atmosphere are indispensable as the natural basis of all
religious education. But in the last analysis only a religious
atmosphere, emanating from the living faith of his teachers,
can reveal the presence of God and make the seed of faith
planted in him at Baptism grow in the child.

Especially for the three- and four-year-old a religious atmosphere is of capital importance and without it it is not
possible to begin with the practice of religious life at this age,
either at home or at school. Silence, respect, a transparent faith
and an inner joy are essential to it.

SILENCE There can be no truly religious activity, that is one
which puts the child into some sort of relationship
with God, without silence and recollection. In this silence the
child's senses are quietened and he becomes capable of perceiving something of the mystery. Stillness is for him an unusual
condition which prepares him to perceive something 'beyond',
something quite different and in this way he can enter into
contact with the mysterious presence of God as far as he is
capable.

All prayer should therefore, if possible, be preceded by a

---

[1] In the programme for the year there are practical suggestions on this point.
Parents should make special note of the suggestions on speaking with dignity
and well-chosen words and the use of discretion before interrupting the
child's activities without serious reason. On the subject of politeness: it
should not be a merely friendly politeness but a loving politeness, for a child
is incapable of friendly politeness unless he has been led to love those to
whom we wish him to be polite.

quietening down and a change over to silence. Each act of religion should be done with special recollection so that the child will come to feel that he is taking part in something privileged. The reading of Bible stories, the recitation of religious poetry and all activities which have something to do with his spiritual development should all be accompanied by this same recollection.

The silence and stillness of churches are most expressive and can help a small child to become recollected; he senses, as it were, an actual presence, and is awed by the grandeur. A hymn, a religious poem, a wax taper, half darkness—all these may be appropriate means to achieving the silence of prayer.[1] In one way or another, everything possible should be done that each day the child may have a short period of real silence filled with the presence of God.

RESPECT To show a special respect for everything which touches religion is another way of preparing the child to meet God.

Nothing impresses a child so much as the regard his parents and teachers have for everything which concerns God and the respect with which they perform religious acts, and usually he will experience real joy in imitating them in this. Silence has already been mentioned; stillness and good posture are other marks of deference.

Respect can also be expressed by the tone of voice, by carefully chosen words (we shall speak of this later), in the religious and aesthetic qualities of the pictures shown, by our deportment and certain liturgical gestures, by the carefulness and seriousness with which we take part in religious ceremonies. When we make some spiritual truth known to him, the child should have the impression that we are revealing something of great value to him. When we speak to him of God, our whole attitude should testify to our faith in the presence and majesty of the

---

[1] Many children can achieve calmness at prayers only by hearing a hymn or by singing their prayers.

Lord. Even on those occasions when we approach these subjects in a more familiar way, the child should always be able to sense our respectfulness.

It is clear that the greater our uncontested prestige in the child's eyes, the more respect he will feel for the religion we reveal to him with so much care.

TRANSPARENT   It should be clearly stated, and we shall often
FAITH   return to this point, that it is only by having a
              living faith ourselves and by having the simplicity to let it shine through before the child that we can spontaneously find the right attitude to adopt with him for his spiritual formation. Only then will the child feel that we are genuine in what we say.

It will be seen when we come to discuss his desire to grow, that the readiness of a child of this age to imitate older people and conform to the environment is not due to a simple reflex which an educator can direct at will in any way he chooses. It is rather the effect of a force in his personality which, in order to develop, selects living examples from those around him to imitate. To find his way, the child needs at first to follow the paths taken by other lives and, especially spiritually, he can make no progress except in contact with the life of another spirit. We should make no mistake here : a genuine religious life will only take root and develop in a child in contact with a living faith and through the influence of the spiritual life of those around him, and not through empty words and gestures. On the contrary, an artificial and stiff attitude will have a disastrous effect on him in the long run.

However, example alone cannot give the faith to a child. Supernatural faith is the fruit of the grace of God. But the activity of the Holy Spirit in the depths of the child's soul is normally conditioned, in accordance with the Divine Will, by the outward testimony of others : 'You will give testimony of me,' said Jesus to his apostles. These words are addressed to all educators associated with the sanctifying work of the Church, and therefore to all parents and teachers in charge of the religious education of children. Only personal witnesses who are bound to the Divine Reality by living faith and love can effectively put the child into a relationship of real faith with the living God.

INNER JOY   The spiritual joy with which our faith and our respect for religion are stamped will succeed in revealing the presence and love of God to the child. Thanks to this, he will come to think of God as a very loving father, as a friend present in his life, as a source of joy, peace and life. The child's adoration will be accompanied by love, filial confidence and thanksgiving. His religion will be expressed by the gift of his whole heart to God, by the desire to be with him and to please him.

Joy should therefore animate us when we evoke the name of God. Let us maintain this joyfulness by meditating carefully on the Divine friendship in which we have a share since our Redemption. Supernatural joy will give clarity to our vision, warmth to our voice, an indefinable joyfulness to our actions : the child will be captivated by it, will eagerly turn to us and, in order to share in this joy, will welcome the God we make known to him.   ·

Recollection and respect, radiant faith and inner joy : to express in one word the kind of atmosphere which is necessary to the child of this age for his religious, as for his merely human development, we can evoke the name of the Blessed Virgin. And in fact, who can better teach us to live in interior peace, honouring God and children, in joyful, active love of God, than the mother of Jesus? Parents and teachers who take their splendid task seriously will turn instinctively to our Lady; they will ceaselessly meditate on her example and ask her help, and when their task is finished they will not forget that it was through her that this grace came to them from God.

HE IS A LITTLE
EXPLORER
EAGER TO DOMINATE

The vital instinct which is at the basis of the child's tendency to reflect his environment reveals itself quite early in the eagerness with which he begins to explore the world of people and things around him. It is here that his need to dominate is most clearly revealed.

Within the scope allowed to him, the child comes and goes ceaselessly : he gets up, gets down, runs, stops—he is indefatigable . . . and often very tiring, especially at the age of four.

Everything interests him, anything excites him and stirs up his curiosity, especially living and moving things. He stops still in front of them and watches them. He goes from one thing to another, touching everything, taking hold of anything within reach.

Moreover, he is unbearable in a living room, and surprisingly happy in a garden. In the open he is free to move as much as he pleases and nature has endless surprises in store for him. There he can spend long periods in which one need not bother with him and every so often he will reappear only to tell of some quite unexpected discovery.

This active exploration of his environment gives him the opportunity to exercise his strength, to capture for himself the world around him—in brief, it gives him the chance of asserting himself.

His liking for play can be explained in the same way. It is the most usual form of activity for a child of this age. Play is not just a kind of relaxation for him—it is his very life. While he plays he feels master of himself and he is continually testing his strength and learning new skills. Play is an occupation to be taken seriously in a child : it is necessary to his growth.

A Definite Frame for the Child's Life

To assert himself the child needs his senses to dominate the world around him, so it would be a mistake to oppose his natural vitality and curiosity on principle. On the contrary he must be allowed to explore. He should be given as much freedom as possible to come and go, to touch things, to play in his own way, to give free rein to the activity of his senses.

It is good if he can have some corner which is just his own— a play room, a passage, a corner of a room, a patch of grass— where he can feel completely at ease, where he can experiment and find subject matter for numerous experiences. Care should be taken that his games are not interrupted without good reason.

Above all, everything should be done to give the child enough contact with nature, which is the ideal setting for his activities.

To help the child put some order into his discoveries and to prepare for the awakening of thought, it is useful to give him educational toys and materials, at home or at school : graded blocks, weights of different sizes, rods of different length, toys of various shades of colour. In this way the child can develop his ability to make distinctions, he will learn to organize his sensations and progress in this will be for him the source of a new and more spiritual joy.

Let us be full of life and enthusiasm ourselves when we are with the child, let him always find us ready to take part in his experiments and to marvel at his discoveries. When we talk to him or show him something, we should be lively, and by using different tones of voice and appropriate gestures we shall make it easier for him to take in what we are putting to him. He should become infected with our own delight and enthusiasm while we are helping him in his discoveries.

RELIGION SHOULD BE PRESENTED IN A CONCRETE AND ACTIVE WAY

God is life. The grace of God, as Jesus said to the Samaritan woman, is a living spring. Religion, then, should not be associated in the child's mind with the living room where he is for-

bidden to move but rather with a garden which promises
innumerable discoveries.[1]

His religion should spring spontaneously from his everyday
life—from his joys, delights, discoveries, from his questions, his
secret desires, his good intentions, from the events of his family
or school life. When, under the stress of some emotion or event,
the child experiences an indefinable longing and sensitivity of
soul, we should know just what to say in order to reveal to
him the God for whom his soul secretly yearns. Thus God will
become the object of his joys, his desires, his whole life.[2]

The child's interest in nature offers another way to make
God known to him. One can take advantage of an occasion
when he delights in the discovery of a flower, a bird, a ray of
sunlight, to lead him from joy in the thing itself to thanksgiving
to God. Some simple words which come naturally to us are
enough, or a short prayer suggested to the child, such as,
'Thank you, Lord', 'Lord we bless you for these beautiful
flowers', 'Lord you have made wonderful things', 'Lord you
are great and beautiful', 'Lord you are good'.

Even his religious life must be alive and full of interest for
the child. It must first of all be active. It should consist of a
definite kind of behaviour, of actions to be done, of tasks to be
accomplished. A feeling or an idea must always correspond to
something active. In giving outward expression to things, a child
can better enter into a mood and can more easily imagine a
scene.[3]

---

[1] This in no way contradicts what we have said about silence and the necessary
part played by stillness and control in all religious life. It is not a question
of a dead silence required by politeness or one not at all adapted to the child
but rather a silence of awe which overcomes the child before something
which impresses and fascinates him. Religious stillness should not be a
constraint imposed habitually on the child's activities, but something
exceptional which impresses and attracts him precisely because of its silence
and forms an essential part of his religious activities.

[2] There are some interesting pages on this subject in Marie Fargues, *La foi
des petits enfants*, (Bloud et Gay, 1950) especially pp. 87-94 and 147-151:
how to raise one's thoughts from pleasure in playing to the love of God.

[3] A child in infant school says the 'Hail Mary' with actions because in this
way, 'one sees the Virgin Mary better'.

Amongst the religious *activities* suitable to this age we suggest, for example—besides the silence before God—a respectful posture during prayers, visits to a church, a little procession in class or at home, a song or a hymn with actions, miming a mystery of religion, colouring a drawing, or a free drawing on a religious subject, picking or giving flowers and arranging them in the oratory, doing some work well for God, an act of kindness to a friend, ready obedience to mother or teacher, an act of charity to the poor.

Religious *stories* can contribute much to a child's wonder of God, and so can short, vivid conversations on spiritual things. They should convey to the child something of the wealth of the supernatural, its inexhaustible joys and unfailing attractions, and at the same time draw him on to action.[1]

Pictures should form part of his familiar world so that he can have the opportunity to encounter once more the things we tell him about : the Crib, the Crucifix, any picture chosen with care and truly religious in expression, on a subject taken from the life of Jesus or the Blessed Virgin, or,—with greater caution, however—from the Old Testament and the lives of the Saints, which can be understood by the child and in some way imitated by him.[2]

[1] Let us make clear that we are not speaking here of those pious stories—unfortunately all too common—which do nothing but charm the imagination and affect the feelings without awakening faith or charity. Nor is it a matter of stories only composed for purposes of instruction, so as to have him cover for example, large tracts of Bible History. We are dealing with stories of a different kind, and we shall give examples later on in the book. We shall also deal later with objections, very widespread nowadays, against the use of stories from the Scriptures in the education of young children.

[2] Certain educators wish to abolish the use of pictures in teaching young children religion on account of their infrequent abuse and the scarcely religious use which is often made of them. However, it seems to us that the possibility of abuse is not sufficient ground to condemn a method of teaching which is so well adapted to the psychology of a child and which, above all, is so traditional in the Church. It would be preferable to point out its positive usefulness.

How, for example, can educators advise the celebration of Christmas with young children, and especially with children from religious families, without the help of a Crib or a picture of the Nativity, when the majority of parents affirm that thanks to the presence of the Crib, Christmas is the very time when it is easiest to create a supernatural atmosphere in the family and to

To keep his interest alive, let us try to introduce changes into the form of his devotions according to the occasion, the feasts or the time of the Liturgical year: a lighted picture, crucifix lowered to be more in evidence, paschal candle, etc.

However it should not be forgotten that all these actions, stories, pictures, have no religious value save through the faith of the person using them and the religious atmosphere in which they are used.

The great religious feasts, which are like landmarks in the liturgical year, are especially appropriate for orienting the child's mind in a definite way towards God and the super-natural. On these occasions activities, stories and pictures, all have a part to play. Moreover, they can illuminate the whole of the child's everyday life and transform it.

The small child will be filled with wonder by the feast of Christmas with the Crib, by Easter preceded by the procession of the palms and the adoration of the Cross, celebrated with joy and light amongst songs and spring flowers, by the feast of the Presentation, with the procession of lights in honour of 'Jesus, Light of the World'—by any of the feasts of the Blessed Virgin, celebrated by a small liturgical ceremony; perhaps even by the feast of Corpus Christi, the Guardian Angels and some patron saints of the family. Each of these feasts can be a really spiritual event: prepared with care, surrounded by respect, filled with joy, it can make God present in the life of the child.[1]

THE CHILD NEEDS WORDS
TO DOMINATE THINGS

At the age of three or four, the child's curiosity turns to a

achieve recollection in prayer? We fear that these educators do not take sufficient account of what a child is at this age—at least the child of today—and deprive themselves of an extraordinary (and possibly very religious) means of conveying the message of Christmas to the child. Have they really never seen the expression of wonder and adoration with which a child, in an atmosphere of faith, contemplates the scene of the Nativity?

[1] On how to present these feasts to the child and how to celebrate them, there are suggestions in the year's programme.

new field : language. Words become for him an important means to domination.

Even when he was small, he loved words. He loved them in themselves and for the pleasure they gave him in articulating and in working at will the strong and supple mechanism of his vocal chords. He could be heard repeating the same syllables over and over again. He was fascinated by the variety of auditory sensations : resonance, rhythm, intensity of sounds. Speech was full of delight for him.

This taste for words stayed with him, and he still likes to roll their resonant syllables around his tongue, but another joy has been added to saying them—that of seeing the image of what he says spring up in his imagination. A word has become a means of securing things for his thoughts.

Before, when one wanted to teach him a word, one could make use only of his instinct to imitate; one said the word, he repeated it. Now he asks for it of his own accord. He seems to have understood that each being has a name which reveals its secret and gives one a hold on it.

A word is now a name, and a name has become the thing itself for him. To speak a name is to create a being in his mind. To tell the child the name of a thing is to give him the means of possessing it in himself. Likewise, the activity of his senses is no longer the only means to domination in his exploration of the world—from now on he sets out to conquer beings by searching for their names.

To learn the names of the things around him becomes one of the principal occupations of this age. In this way can be explained the majority of a child's 'Why's'. At three and four years of age they rarely express interest in a real cause but rather his need to know names and the desire to hear them said once more—when it is not, even more simply, to satisfy his need to talk, to show his presence or to attract attention.

Once a child has a name in his 'possession' he starts to use it and repeat it. He feels that in speaking of something he acquires an increasing mastery and a more certain possession of the thing itself. When at last he has truly mastered the name, the thing truly belongs to him and is part of his personal possessions. It is his way of coming to know and appropriating everything little by little.

THE CHILD NEEDS WORDS TO MAKE HIS DISCOVERIES HIS OWN

As the child needs words to master the world around him, he needs to be talked to : let us explain what we are doing, describe what we see, let us tell him what things are called. In this way, with our help, he will widen his field of conquest and strengthen his discoveries.

Let us also tell him innumerable little stories to teach him about things, but always with well chosen words, simply and expressively, in the tone of natural conversation and not in baby talk. A child of three or four is no longer a baby.

It is not always easy to accept a child's questions gracefully, especially when he has already asked them twenty times. This is the right method, all the same. The child is not yet ready for school, but he can learn a great deal from these occasional lessons which crop up as we answer his questions.

In doing this, we should try to satisfy the exact need which his questions express : he should not be puzzled with explanations when all he wants is a clear short statement, nor overwhelmed with lots of new words when he wants only to hear us repeat some familiar words he has used himself.

When we explain the meaning of a word, it is very helpful to show him the thing we are talking about. The connection between the thing and its name will be much more surely established and the child more satisfied with his discovery.

As well as this, we should acquire the knack of using words which appeal to a child's ear. The fascination of a word, a resonant phrase or rhythm, sometimes helps him to accept with a smile an otherwise painful situation. There are key words such as 'big', 'beautiful', 'good', 'surprise', 'secret'. We should not be afraid to repeat the same phrases often like a rhythmical refrain. Little poems and rhymes will delight him.

The child must also be allowed to talk freely himself. He should be allowed to get carried away by words even if we are tired of listening to him. In this way, he will gradually make the vocabulary of those around him his own and his capacity for thinking will be increased by an extraordinary number of new acquisitions. Our attention while he talks will encourage him to speak and express himself well, and in listening to him we shall come to know him better.

RELIGIOUS WORDS TO INTRODUCE HIM TO SPIRITUAL THINGS

To come to know God and spiritual things, the child needs to hear them spoken of and to speak of them himself. Only under these conditions can the seed of faith, implanted in him at Baptism, grow in the child. Did not God himself reveal himself to men by speaking as well as doing and did he not command his Church to awaken the faith in the hearts of men by transmitting his Word?

SPEAK OF GOD TO THE CHILD We must take advantage of the opportunities which present themselves to express our faith before the child, and he should be allowed to express his. We should comment briefly, for example, on the pictures, the religious symbols we happen to see, on our deportment and the gestures we make during prayers, on feasts celebrated at home or at school. The child should be allowed to talk on these occasions and we should react sympathetically to what he has to say, and we should let him express freely the thoughts which come to his mind when he is performing some act of religion.

If necessary, we should ask questions in order to draw a personal reaction from him. What we tell him, whether it is planned or spontaneous, will familiarize him gradually with

religious truths and teach him the vocabulary of spiritual
things.

TRULY RELIGIOUS   On these occasions we should never use
LANGUAGE   childish language which detracts from
                  the dignity of religion. How can a young
child come to know the sacred and extraordinary character of
the supernatural, the majesty and transcendence of God, if only
his childish words are used? On the contrary, let us try to approach as nearly as possible the language of God in the Scriptures and that of the Church in the Liturgy.

A child is attracted by what is great and he is sensitive to
the evocative power of words. He is impressed by the majesty
of God's language in the Bible and in the prayer of the Church.
Their solemnity is a highly effective way of introducing him
to sacred things and of making him realize the great majesty of
God. In its language, the Church gives a lesson to those who
adopt a sweet and sentimental way of speaking of religious
things.

Let us call God, 'God' or 'the Lord', and not only 'dear
God'. In our prayers let us say 'Lord God' rather than 'my
God'. Let us speak of 'Jesus Christ' or 'the Lord Jesus' and not
only of 'dear Jesus' or 'sweet Jesus'. Above all do not let us
reduce God to the level of 'baby Jesus'. Neither the Gospels
nor the Liturgy know the expression: they make use of the
term 'Child' which does not exclude the idea of majesty as the
word 'baby' does.[1]

A church may be called the 'House of God', 'the Lord's
House', the altar, 'the Table of the Lord Jesus', a scene taken
from the Bible can be presented as a story taken from 'the
Book of God's Word'. When we talk of spiritual things we can
borrow the words of the Gospel, and instead of saying, 'Jesus
said, "Be kind to everyone" ', why not say, 'The Lord Jesus

---

[1] On the expression 'baby Jesus', see what is said on p. 103. The entire third
part of this book is an illustration of what we say here on religious
language.

said, "Love one another as I have loved you" '—speaking expressively and if necessary, the first time, with some words of explanation?

For many, this will seem revolutionary, but in fact it is only a return to the purest tradition, faithful to the teaching methods of the Church. In every case, experience has shown that this bears much fruit in the religious life of the child ... and of those educating him. A transforming note of respect and majesty is introduced. Only the first step is difficult.

THE CHILD'S   To help the child pray—and again, we say
PRAYER   this at the risk of further scandalizing some
               parents and teachers—we should learn to draw
on the same sources, namely the Bible and the Liturgy, and particularly on the Psalms, the prayers inspired by God himself, whose rhythmical, poetic form has been proved by experience to be perfectly adapted to the young child, if the language is slightly simplified here and there. Beside the prayers which a child says using his own words, let us teach him to pray with the words of the Church.

This kind of prayer is possible only where the adult's own attitude of awe and respect helps the child to come into contact with a God of great majesty. It becomes quite natural to the child who has come to know God through the wonders of Creation or has learnt to adore him through contact with the Scriptures presented as we have suggested in our programme for the year. We think this statement will become clearer to the reader as he progresses with this book.[1]

Children thus prepared can be made to repeat some simple phrases slowly, some verses with corresponding actions, in an atmosphere of silence and respect. For example, 'Lord, my God, you are great and beautiful!' (circular gesture); 'The

[1] The reader should see Appendix 2 (pp. 175-8) where he will see the simple and evocative way in which Soeur St Ignace introduces small children to the prayer 'Holy, holy, holy . . .' The topic of children's prayers is more thoroughly treated on pp. 112-117.

earth and all it contains is yours, Lord' (wide gesture); 'Let us sing to the Lord, for he is good' (hands on the heart) 'for he loves us forever' (arms outstretched); 'To you, O Lord, I lift my heart' (raise hands slowly), 'to you, I lift my arms' (lift arms); 'God is the Lord' (hands joined), 'the great Lord of heaven and earth' (great circular gesture); 'Lord you are holy, holy, holy' (bowing down lower and lower) 'heaven and earth are full of your glory' (or 'your majesty'—great circular gesture); 'Hosannah in the highest!' (hands raised up).

When it is necessary to simplify certain phrases and expressions for children—and it is often necessary—it should be done with discretion and as far as possible keeping to the spirit of the phrases and the poetry of the original words.

Many parents and teachers will be unwilling to accept this advice, in spite of everything we have said to recommend it, and will not attempt to put it into practice either because they think the child incapable of this kind of prayer or because they themselves will not feel at home with this kind of religious language. They should try to introduce it gradually, under the conditions that we have suggested. They will be surprised with the result. That is the language of religion which was given by God, the only one authenticated by the Church, which she uses in her official prayer (the Missal, the Breviary). Used with faith, it is blessed by God.

In drawing on the twofold source of Bible and Liturgy, it will be easy to enrich the child's religious life with prayers varied according to the different times of the year and the sentiments he wants to express: admiration, adoration, praise, thanksgiving, offering, confidence, supplication.[1] A child should be allowed to chant his prayers in the form of psalms or simple rhymes.

Care should be taken with the choice of words, that none of their sounds suggest fanciful meanings which have nothing to

---

[1] They will be helped in this by little books like Abbé Colomb, *Parlez, Seigneur* (Paris) or Mlle Dingeon, *La Prière de l'Eglise et nos enfants* (Paris, 1950).

do with religion. Generally speaking, we should accompany what we say with all sorts of other forms of expressiveness (gestures, tone of voice, facial expressions) which will help the child to grasp the meaning and seriousness of what we are telling him. Afterwards, children should be allowed to talk so that we can find out what they have understood.

Finally, it should be observed—and this is of capital importance—that it is our faith more than the words we use that matters. Someone who uses very imperfect language but has a sincere faith has more chance of making a child conscious of God than one whose language is correct but has not enough faith or conviction or love of God.[1]

HE IS A LITTLE KING

IN A WORLD MADE BY

HIS IMAGINATION

The impression that the child has of having power over things once he knows their names is founded on reality up to a certain point, but it is mainly a figment of his imagination. At this age his imagination plays a very important part in his conquest of the world around him and his assertion of himself. It gives him, in particular, the power to construct for himself a special universe and allows him to develop in the external world with the ease of a little 'magician-king'.

Let us look closely at the way this marvellously creative faculty works, the better to understand the resources which it offers and the precautions it demands for his education.[2]

To sum up what was said earlier, the imagination represents things to the child in such a vivid way that the pictures it gives

[1] On the gravity of our words when speaking of God and on the way to talk to small children, there are interesting suggestions in *La Foi des petits enfants*, by Mme Fargues (Bloud et Gay, Paris, 1950) esp. pp. 36-51.

[2] This rather scientific approach to the child's imagination will perhaps frighten some hurried readers. They should be reassured: the chapters which come later are shorter and easier to read. However, they should not neglect to read this section, which is important if one is to understand the child and the special world in which he usually lives.

him seem to him as real as the world outside. This imaginative capacity, which enables him to build up a personal universe, comes from the mysterious and surprising ability which his childish imagination has of changing reality into what he imagines it to be and at the same time of changing that image itself according to what reality is—in a word to identify himself with it.

THE CHILD   Through his imagination, first of all, the
CHANGES REALITY   child projects into things a *life* like his
                   own. He gives a soul and human feelings to things in nature and to animals he talks to. Psychologists call this the 'animist' phase in a child.

In this way, the external world takes on life and form in his thought, each thing becomes more definite and personal, receives an identity. This identity is still no more than a picture accompanied by a name and certain impressions, but it prepares for the idea that the child will later make of things, and is like a living sketch. Without this image, reality would not exist for him most of the time : image and reality often become confused for him. This is why a word, by the image it brings up in his thought, has for him the value of a thing.

Through his imagination the child also projects onto the world his feelings, which are themselves a reflection of his environment and the result of his education. Everything he feels, whether real or imaginary, becomes somehow transposed into a certain key. If his environment, his past and his temperament predispose him to joy and confidence, everything will take on a sunny aspect and appear marvellous and full of happiness in his eyes. If, on the contrary, he feels frustrated and lives in fear, everything will take on sombre colours and a menacing appearance.

And finally, the child projects his *desires* into things. This allows him to model the real, or rather the idea that he has made of the things around him, to his liking. A stick readily becomes a horse for the boy who is riding it, because the child aspires to grow big and wants to experience the joy of mastering a horse. A few rags are enough to give a little girl the idea that she is splendidly dressed, because she wants to be as beautiful as some young woman that she has admired. Her doll attracts her so much because it gives her the illusion of being a mother. It could be said that as the child is incapable of getting his wish concretely, he makes amends to himself by creating an illusion which is even more satisfying than the real thing could be.

By projecting these innumerable fantasies into the real world, transforming it in every way, the child makes himself an interior universe where dreams are real, and reality pervaded by dreams. Although the child is constantly by our side he is part of another world where nothing and no one is the same for him as it is for us.

The satisfactions which a child procures for himself in this way through his imaginative life, especially in his games, are often illusory as to the exterior object which they represent; but his imagination offers opportunities to exercise his mind and his will and builds up his self-confidence through the world it has fashioned for him, and it is here that he finds very real satisfactions and definite joys.

THE CHILD IDENTIFIES WITH OTHERS The exploits of our little 'magician' do not stop here. He is not satisfied with transforming reality according to his liking—his imagination allows him to change himself according to reality as he perceives it, that is, to *identify himself* with it. Who has not seen a child absorbed in some performance or in a story that is being read to him? He has then become one with the thing he is absorbed in through the pictures which his imagination gives him of it.

Many children's games are founded on a spontaneous identification of this kind with persons, real or imaginary. If he is told a story of a little bird, the child identifies himself with it, flies, sings with it and snuggles into a warm nest with it.

This is why he takes such pleasure in listening to stories. Another time he will be a little rabbit or Tom Thumb. The bear that growls in the forest and makes all the small animals tremble will represent his father (perhaps) or some teacher who is too severe and lacking in gentleness. This will not prevent his furry teddy bear from being the personification of friendliness and an inseparable companion.

All the child's life is thus spent in identifying himself successively with different real and imaginary people and things around him. In the greater part of his activities he unconsciously identifies himself with some other person—his father, his mother, older brother, teacher, a train, an aeroplane, etc. By this procedure, he enriches himself from the life around him, experiences the world and makes the personalities of others his own; above all, he learns to discover himself and tries out his own personality.

The role of the imagination in the life of the child is manifold and of capital importance, as one can see. It serves him not only to create a fairy world and to people his interior universe with the images he needs in order to develop but also to represent the real actively to himself; it makes him exercise himself in conquering little by little the world around him, and allows him to assert and discover himself more and more.

THE CHILD'S WORLD   At this age however, imagination and reality are not radically opposed to each other, but are combined in his thought. It would often be more correct to speak of an imaginative than an imaginary life in connection with the child. Actually, the particular world which is constructed by his imagination is usually neither completely real nor completely imaginary. It starts out from reality, but becomes more or less transformed as it passes through the child's imagination and gets more or less mixed with subjective sentiments, animism and fantasy. Up to a certain point it is all the result of his imagination and bears its mark; but it is not necessarily only imaginary.

It is true that there exists for the child another more realistic world besides the one he constructs for himself, which will overtake the other one, step by step. This is the world of his daily experiences, of material reality whose inertia and fixed laws resist his imagination, of other wills which oppose his own. However, at this age, the world he imagines takes a predominant part in his thoughts. Actually the child has an absolute need for it, partly as protection for his personality, partly as an expression of his vitality and for the satisfaction of certain spiritual needs :

—as *protection* : because, but for the construction of a world whose king he is, he would feel tortured by the hard realities of life and adults. Only later will his eyes slowly open, and by then he will be strong enough to be less hurt by reality;

—as the *expression of his vitality* : the child possesses an extraordinary reservoir of all sorts of potentialities; some will develop later, but from now on they will appear mixed with lots of others in the incessant flow of his imagination;

—as *satisfaction of certain spiritual needs* : the child cannot be satisfied with the material world and his spirit carries him towards a world which is more perfect, where matter faithfully obeys the spirit, where the laws of gravity and locality lose their rigidity; towards an ideal world where his desire for happiness and perfection can be fulfilled—the world of the absolute, the only one which can satisfy him completely.

Far from being the sign of weakness of mind or lack of experience, his imaginative life is evidence of a spiritual nature in the child, a mark of his humanity. Animals are lacking in this. It is part of the charm of a small child and contributes greatly to his worth as an adult later. It is a treasure to be safeguarded, as great personalities, who often envy him this paradise they have lost, know well.

However, this imagination which transforms reality so marvellously and is so good at producing illusions, is not entirely without its dangers. Its limitations must be known and precautions taken.

LET US HELP THE CHILD BUILD A UNIVERSE WHICH HELPS HIM DEVELOP

An educator who fails to take into account the imaginative character of the child's thinking and ignores the special world in which he develops is in danger of being clumsy and deluding himself as to the educative value of his words and actions. He runs the risk of being cut off from a great part of the child's life and deprives himself of many valuable resources.

We should know that, at this age, an idea is grasped only when it is presented as an image. The child will understand what 'politeness' is if the word 'polite' becomes associated with something seen or a story heard or actions done involving politeness. A 'shoemaker' will be for him a man 'like daddy', who hits the soles of shoes with a hammer to repair them or uses a sewing machine 'like mummy' with coarse thread and large needles. If we want to give him the idea of a feeling, like joy or enthusiasm, the images must be given by our gestures and facial expressions.

But which one of us can tell when he talks to a group of children what images will be evoked in their imaginations by the words he uses? They will all be so different! The only way to find out is to let them express themselves straight afterwards, to observe their play, their drawings, their life amongst themselves.

If it is kept in mind that the child has the ability to identify himself with others and if good use is made of this, then he can be greatly influenced. We can be living examples for him and we can encourage him to identify himself with persons who will influence him for the good. Later we shall see the important practical applications of this when we discuss this tendency to imitate the people around him.[1]

Earlier we discussed the attitude to take to his play activities. The importance of toys and stories in a child's life should be understood.

[1] See pp. 60-4.

A little girl should not be deprived of the pleasure of having a doll (not too big), nor the little boy of his bear (not too bulky); the child living in town should be allowed to have a small private kingdom of familiar toys (simple and solid ones), which will provide him with numerous opportunities to assert his personality and to develop.[1]

A story stimulates a child's phantasy and liveliness. It allows him to live out adventures in his thoughts which make him feel big and extends the field of his experience. The child needs to be given food for his imagination. He greedily takes in all the images presented to him, puts life into them, transforms them, but he is hardly capable of inventing any new one by himself. Stories enrich his interior world. It is up to us to give him this enjoyment.

The stories a child likes best are the ones where they encounter familiar experiences, stories about other children, animals, well-known things, or about impressive and slightly mysterious personalities and also those which take him beyond his experience and beyond this world.

At the age of three, children especially like stories which deal with experiences like their own. Stories about animals fascinate them. We can invent stories about persons like 'Mr Yes-yes' who has all sorts of pleasant adventures and a 'Mr No-no' who is always in trouble. One single word from a story of this sort can often be enough to put the child in a good mood.

At four, a particularly imaginative and exuberant age, we should add stories about growing: 'Little Seed' who has the courage to stay in the dark earth until she starts to grow and grow and break through the ceiling of her house, to become a beautiful green plant and later a huge tree which gives shelter to thousands of little creatures in its branches; stories for his imagination about trains, cars, ships, aeroplanes, birds, little people seeking adventure; stories where truth is mixed with

---

[1] Toys are also a sign for the child of his parents' love for him and play a large part in the child's emotional life.

invention like the story of Babar the Elephant; and finally, purely imaginary stories like fairy tales.

When we tell a child stories, we should keep in mind that we are trying to help him build up a world for himself which is habitable and which helps him to develop. We should watch for the effect that the words, images, stories told to him produce. Sometimes it takes very little to make a child anxious and frightened.[1]

One must also learn to listen to children when they tell stories in their own way. They should be encouraged to draw and to explain what they have drawn.[2] We should watch them play and not disdain to take part in their games some-times. In this way we can gradually enter into the child's world, and be accepted as a friend and useful ally in building it up. A child who sees an adult bending down to him and enter-ing into his world with sympathy will be more than ready to follow him later with enthusiasm.

On the other hand, the child should not be allowed to shut himself up entirely in his own private world or, even worse, in a world of pure fantasy. His sense of reality must be gradu-ally awakened. Some prudent appeals to his critical sense will prove useful in an obviously extreme case. This must be done in a pleasant manner, without shaking his self-confidence and without destroying his pleasure in believing what he is told. On the contrary, it should provide him with the added pleasure of getting to know new things. Bit by bit, the child himself will start distinguishing between what is real and what is imagin-ary in his own world.

LET US HELP THE CHILD TO ACQUIRE A TRUE IDEA OF RELIGION

From a certain point of view, the child's imagination is like

---

[1] There is, however, an educative way of utilizing some frightening stories (see pp. 81-2).
[2] On how to receive drawings done by the child and their deep significance see P. Etavard, *Maman, comprends-moi* (Editions Ouvrières, Paris, 1955) pp. 197-204.

a door opening out on the supernatural, and we have to help the child to open it onto an authentic religious world.

The child does not need abstract ideas; explanations will not introduce him to the reality of the supernatural. Examples accompanied by impressions will do that better than anything else.

These examples have to be chosen with great care. The child must be able to understand them, they have to correspond somehow to his own experience and they must appeal to him; but, above all, they must evoke the supernatural in all its truth without distorting it. Here are some examples.

VIVID   For example, the child should come to know the
EXAMPLES   invisible, spiritual presence of God, though see-
                 ing the attitude of his parents at prayer, watching
their gestures reflecting their consciousness of God's omni-present majesty and goodness, and through hearing the loving respect in their tone of voice when they pronounce the name of God.

The child should feel the presence of the Lord when he hears the story of Moses on the mountain being called by God from the burning bush, or the story of Samuel hearing himself called by name several times during the night.[1] He should sense the majesty of the Child in the Crib through seeing the adults around him join with the Three Kings in adoration.

It should not be thought that examples taken from the past and from stories should be banned. On the contrary, they can strengthen the child's, and even our own faith. A child looks at the past in the same way as he looks at the present, an historic figure can mean just as much to him as somebody around him, a story can be just as real as a present action. It is enough if the adult believes the event of the past that he is telling, and presents it vividly with sincere faith under appropri-

---

[1] A good presentation of these two stories can be found in H. Lubienska de Lenval, *L'education du sens religieux*, (Paris, 1946) pp. 36 and 38. We ourselves give a version adapted to small children of the first of these episodes (pp. 129 ff.).

ate conditions—in a word, if he himself participates in it. It is also important that the story be such that the child can apply it in some way to his own life, so that with the help of grace it will cease to be merely a past event pictured in the imagination but will become something rooted in present real faith.

We have to choose examples carefully, so that they are valid for everyone—adults as well as children—and have authentic religious value, that is to say, give the child the opportunity to come into contact with God through faith, imbued with adoration and love.

EXAMPLES REVEALED   We should therefore look to the Bible
BY GOD   for examples and likenesses which God himself used to reveal himself, and use them to make God known to children in the same way. Depending on the situation, we can use the images of light or clouds, lightning or night, the noise of thunder or silence, the light breeze or the powerful wind, of a watchfulness over our actions or the voice which calls and speaks to us, of some of God's miraculous actions, of the apparition of a frightening or mysterious angel, of the powerful or delicate beauty of something in creation. Above all we must bring the child into close contact with the humanity, deeds and mysteries of the life of our Lord Jesus, in whom the 'light of God's glory' is resplendent.

We should also point out how great religious men reacted to these manifestations of God : Moses taking off his shoes and covering his face with his cloak with awe before God, Samuel readily answering God's call with 'Lord, I am here !', Abraham's faith in God's word, David's confidence when fighting Goliath, Solomon's offering to God a magnificent Temple, St Francis of Assisi's joyful thanksgiving for the creation and, above all, the attitude of our Lord himself. The example of these truly religious gestures will bring an atmosphere of grandeur and goodness to the child's religious life.

It serves no purpose to introduce many different episodes

and persons: it is better if the children in our charge become
more familiar with only a few which seem to suit them particularly well. The stories should offer them examples of feelings they too could experience, definite attitudes which they
could adopt in presenting themselves to God and which, as
far as possible, they can find reflected in the religious life of
those around them.

In this way they will come to appreciate the story of God's
people and the life of Jesus' friends, they will feel themselves
becoming another Moses or David, they will join the shepherds
at the Crib, the Three Kings, the Apostles, they will want to
identify themselves with the Blessed Virgin, the saints and the
Lord Jesus himself.

THE IMAGE   While trying to adapt ourselves to the child's
OF GOD   mind, we should be careful not to belittle God in
             his thought, and we should be particular about
the religious quality of the examples we present. The invisible
and spiritual God of the Old Testament or the 'Heavenly
Father, who sees all things' but whom we cannot see in this
life, should not be represented in a material way, nor should
God be reduced to the person of Jesus only.

The word 'God' should evoke an image of a spiritual presence
in the child's mind, one that is magnificent and to be wor-
shipped, but at the same time lovable and very near, as the
result of the various examples drawn from nature, from the
Old and the New Testaments and the influence of extraordinary or familiar (but always authentic) impressions drawn
from his own life or that of those around him, or the life of
some saint.

We must realize that for a child, what counts when they
are together is not so much the physical appearance of the
person he loves but the benefit he gets from his presence; the
feeling of being loved and appreciated, of being bigger, more
assured and capable of doing more because the loved one is
there. A person present to him, by his side, means someone

taking an interest in what he is doing, someone talking to and helping him; the knowledge that that person is by him gives him more self-confidence and security, creates an atmosphere of sympathy, love and joy.

This gives us valuable indications as to how we should introduce him to God, Jesus, the Blessed Virgin, the angels and saints and the relationship which should exist between the child and the supernatural. If we speak of these persons as the Bible and the Liturgy do, using the same words and with the same sobriety and awe, surrounding them with the same respect as Church does in the Liturgy, the child, who can with great facility conceive of beings independent of material laws, will be amazed to discover the existence of a supernatural world, to learn that he is surrounded by invisible beings who support and protect him.

THE SUPERNATURAL   Confusion between the 'supernatural'
AND MAGIC   and 'magic' in the child's mind must be
                     avoided, and the examples we use
(stories, pictures, suggested activities) must be chosen for their *religious value* and not for their picturesque character. What they must do is help the child form an idea of the real and living presence of God in a spiritual manner, so that he spontaneously adopts a religious attitude before it.

In considering such episodes as that of the serpent in the Garden of Eden, the plague of frogs in Egypt, the changing of Lot's wife into a pillar of salt, the exploits of Samson, Jonas and the whale, etc., we should ask ourselves how these could be useful to his religious life. With children of this age, it is preferable to make use of episodes where God himself shows himself to man, talks to him, comes to his aid.

Nor should a religious story be presented in the same way, with the same atmosphere, as an invented story. We should particularly avoid the presentation of miracles which approach purely magic acts, especially as this does not make God seem superior to man to a child who attributes magic powers to himself and others with great ease. A miracle, just like any religious story, should be presented above all as a mystery in which God manifests himself in his majesty and love. Miracles should be talked about with seriousness but the examples we tell the child should not be too numerous, in order to avoid giving him a wrong idea of God's activity in his life. Nonetheless, a place of importance does need to be given to them, for the truly miraculous as manifested in certain of God's actions can reveal the mystery of a divine presence with particular force to the child.

At first the child cannot distinguish reality from invention in a story, and it is useless to explain that one story actually happened and another is invented. This will make no sense to him. But it is already possible and necessary to make a distinction between the two fields by the different treatment given to a religious story in telling the facts and giving descriptions, by the seriousness with which it is told, and the conclusions drawn from it for the child's (and the grown-up's) life. A lot of imagination can be used in the telling of a fairy-tale, but not in the telling of an episode from the Gospels, which is of a different quality, and must be accompanied by love, respect, prayer, self-offering. One does not expect the child to love Little Red Riding Hood, or to pray for or like Thom Thumb, but then *he will not see his parents kneel down before them.* A child will register these differences unconsciously and later it will come naturally to him to make the same distinction.

If the supernatural is presented to him in this way, it will lead not to the creation of an unreal world in his thoughts but to the discovery of a spiritual universe actually surrounding him, and not only himself, but those around him also. This revelation will correspond, not to the need he feels to protect himself by illusions against the hardships of reality, which is a temporary one later to be discarded, but to that thirst for the infinite and the divine which grace gives him and which should stay with him through his whole life, because it is a mark in the depth of his soul of his vocation as a child of God.

THE CHILD
ATTRIBUTES ABSOLUTE TRUTH TO
EVERYTHING HE IS TOLD

The child's readiness to believe unconditionally anything he is told with assurance makes it all the more necessary to exercise the discrimination we have just discussed. This credulity is the mark of a spirit made for truth and for the absolute. The child of this age needs to believe that everything is true. He thinks of and accepts things as if they were absolute, and he turns this into yet another way of asserting himself.

It is his natural instinct to cling strongly to any thought, image or word presented to him and he takes advantage of any opportunity to assert both inwardly and to others, 'It is true. I believe it.' So, added to the satisfaction of being absolutely certain of some truth, he has the satisfaction of exercising his power of thought by pronouncing absolute judgment.

He will be even more prepared to accept as absolute truth everything he is told by an adult who has his entire confidence and whom he believes to be infallible. A child likes to repeat what a grown-up tells him with an assurance which simply does not know the possibility of doubt. The joy this gives him is even greater when what the grown-up says corresponds to his deepest desires, especially his desire to grow, his need for love and for the absolute.

SPECIAL REGARD FOR TRUTH WITH A CHILD

We must understand this need the child has to believe in the reality of what he imagines and the truth of what he thinks, and his spontaneous remarks should be listened to with seriousness and goodwill, no matter how naïve they are. His illusions should not be brutally taken from him, but with the help of the confidence he has in us, he should be led tactfully, step by step, towards reality as it is. On the other hand, when what he says corresponds to the truth, we should take care to show our approval.

We must be perfectly loyal to the child and not abuse his credulity. His confidence in us demands this. There is a difference between telling him fascinating stories and maintaining seriously the truth of inexact statements, and when he really asks questions we should always give him true answers.[1]

When we are speaking to a child of this age, we should adopt a positive tone and express ourselves simply, clearly and with conviction, so that he can make what we tell him his own and repeat it himself, for he needs to believe and affirm in order to develop. If what we tell him corresponds to his aspirations towards what is great, beautiful, lovable and extraordinary, if it fulfils his desire for love and for the absolute, the child will nourish himself from our convictions and will find there a deep and lasting joy.

TRUTH TO NOURISH HIS FAITH

A baptized child, over and above his natural tendency to believe everything, feels a supernatural attraction for everything which concerns God. Baptism has put in him a sort of 'divine instinct of faith', a forceful belief in his Lord, coming from God himself, which often enough becomes a tangible attraction to the supernatural.

Let us therefore take this child's religion seriously. We should not treat his questions and his worries on the subject of religion lightly, and we should respect his naïveté and simple faith. What he says, and the conviction with which he prays and does other religious acts should be received with gravity by those around him, and his older brothers and sisters should not be allowed to make fun of his youth and naturalness.

We, for our part, must see to the truth of everything we tell the child in the course of his religious education—in the words

---

[1] Note what is said on this point, with regard to Christmas, on p. 138 ff.

we use, the stories we tell him, the answers and explanations we give him—so that his religion will have a solid foundation and so that, as he grows older, he may have to discard nothing of the faith of his childhood, but on the contrary may recognize that his teachers have given him from his youth imperishable food, the authentic Word of God.

As the child of three and four needs statements rather than explanations, we should tell him with certainty and clarity what we want to teach him in God's name. Let us tell him the simple and essential truths of religion : God is great, God is strong, God is beautiful, more so than any other being—God is good, God loves us, God is with us, God is our Father in heaven,[1] God sees everything, God knows everything, God loves what is good, and does not love what is bad—it is God who has given us everything we have, he has given us the Lord Jesus—Jesus is the Son of God, he is our great Friend, the Friend of all men, he came to earth to help us—he died for us and rose again after three days—he is living in heaven, but he is also with us, his friends on earth, helping us.

The child should come to know these truths one by one and should be made to affirm them also. If he hears us repeat them with faith, he will naturally make them his own with the same faith. And in affirming them himself he will experience the human joy of mastering with assurance an absolute truth— the joy of a faith which God himself will confirm within him.

[1] On the precautions to be taken when calling God 'Father' see p. 102, note 1.

2 THE CHILD NEEDS A RELIGION WHICH WILL HELP HIM DEVELOP

WITH THREE- to four-year-olds, the way of asserting themselves against grown-ups is even more characteristic than their eagerness to explore the world. This need for self-assertion makes itself very obvious. The child admires those bigger than himself, he wants to raise himself to their level. He has a real yearning to grow, and use must be made of this to encourage the child's development. On the religious level we should tell the child, so eager by nature and by grace to grow, that God is great and wishes to see him develop and grow in every way.

For the child of this age the simplest way of equating himself to grown-ups is to imitate their behaviour. The child is eager to do this and he needs examples he can imitate. In his religious education he needs living example, especially that of our own religious life.

But in order to feel big, the child also needs the approbation of adults. He must have the support of our encouragement and approval, and as a child of God he needs to learn of the loving presence of his Lord, who is actively interested in his life and who approves of the good he does.

Finally, his desire to feel equal to grown-ups induces him to accept, and even to like, submitting to certain rules and prohibitions of the adult world. This will help us in making the child set his life in a framework of discipline which will give it something of the glory of the grown-up's life. In his religious life, in the same way, he can come to understand that by imposing certain demands on himself, as a young Christian should, he can make his life more pleasing to God.

THE CHILD LONGS
TO GROW

At the age of three and four, on every possible occasion the child's behaviour expresses this desire to grow. He is full of his own importance, acts with great dignity, takes himself seriously, and there are already signs of a certain self-love. He is pleased and satisfied with himself and behaves as though he were the centre of the universe.

His parents will notice his desire to decide for himself, his taste for doing things 'all by himself', especially at home where he is more familiar with the persons in charge of him and with the jobs to be done.

This assertiveness is not without friction with those around him, and especially with his brothers and sisters. The younger does not want to be inferior to the older and the older wants to dominate the younger.

It should be noted that the child's discovery of 'I' and 'me' (his own person and will) is usually accompanied by the discovery of the sex to which he belongs, and he becomes conscious of the differences which exist between the sexes. The boy experiences a certain pride. He begins to identify himself with 'men' and associates himself with his father, as the girl does with her mother.

The child is also interested in babies. This interest is explainable by the attraction which everything living has for him, but even better, perhaps, by the feeling of superiority which he experiences with someone smaller than himself, in a world where his age keeps him in a position inferior to those around him.

This desire to grow, finally, explains at least in part the pleasure he takes in nature, especially in growing plants and animals.

HELPING THE CHILD TO GROW

This eagerness to grow is of great assistance to those concerned with the child's education, and they will do well to take this 'little man' seriously. They can make constant use of his desire by presenting what requires effort as a means to growing up.

The child's initiative is to be encouraged and his spontaneity respected. He should be allowed to do things 'all by himself'. We should not be too shocked by his outbursts of violence, cheekiness, recklessness or excessive exuberance. We shall discuss later, when dealing with his need to conform, how far it is possible and desirable to put limits on his liberty and spontaneity, for his own good and in the name of this very desire to grow.

Anything which could give the child a feeling of inferiority should generally be avoided, especially unfavourable comparisons with others. At this age, it is not good to point out the child's faults. Far from encouraging him, this most often robs him of any desire to improve and any inclination towards good.[1]

By our behaviour, by carefully choosing our words and the tone we use, we can influence the child without his realizing

[1] It has already been noted that children will naturally identify themselves with their parents. However, it should also be remarked that it is the home atmosphere which determines which parent the child will prefer to identify himself with, and the mutual love and respect which exists between his parents is of capital importance in making such an identification work for his good. In a home where one parent belittles or despises the other, the child will automatically (at first, at any rate), want to identify himself with the 'stronger', even when he is of a different sex. If, on top of this, there is an implication that this inferiority is due inevitably to the sex of the person ('Women are stupid', 'Men are a bad and selfish lot') the child will most assuredly experience conflict and anxiety—feeling himself inevitably destined by his sex to an inferior role. (This is often the case with girls.) What is important is that each sex has a dignity and worth of its own in spite, or because, of the differences which exist between them (which at this age is best conveyed by the parent's attitude to one another). If in a family boys are more proud of being boys than the girls are of being girls (or vice versa), then there is something wrong. (Translator's note.)

it, gradually to have respect for the private parts of his body.[1]
At this age, the child should be given the opportunity of learning how children of the opposite sex are made, for example
when a baby is having a bath at home or, if this is not possible,
at the home of friends or relatives. An elementary knowledge
of the anatomy of the sexes is *necessary* for the normal education of a child.

The law of growth in living things, plants and animals can
be pointed out in nature and, by analogy, many children of
four to five years, especially in larger families, can understand
how a baby can grow in its mother's body from a seed like that
of a fruit in the calyx of a flower. If this is explained with delicacy, it can be something very beautiful for a child.

A child should get used to treating babies gently; he should
learn to control his liveliness and to transform his desire to
dominate into a need to protect and help those who are weaker.

We can best help the child to develop by being 'big' in his
eyes ourselves. The more esteem and respect the child has for
us, the more will our words and behaviour influence him. An
adult without authority and prestige cannot educate a child of
this age who wants to grow and needs to find someone big to
look up to.

The Greatness of God and His Desire to See the Child Grow

But grace gives to the young Christian an added secret

---

[1] If the child makes a rude gesture he should not be stopped with the words,
'That's dirty' because he will then think of his body as something dirty.
On the contrary it is better to say 'A big boy doesn't do that. He respects
himself'. The child will then think of himself with respect and will get into
the habit of treating himself with dignity.

Some teachers do not pay enough attention to this aspect of education,
and it sometimes happens even in kindergarten that certain abuses between
children develop (notably in dressing rooms) without the teacher's awareness. Some children need to be told in class how to behave. This should be
done with discretion and delicacy, but with clarity and the same simplicity
as would be used in speaking of matters of hygiene, *without ever making use of
threats*.

attraction to the greatness of God, a more penetrating feeling for the mystery which is beyond him, a more pronounced longing for perfection, for the absolute and the infinite.

This child, attracted as he is by everything great, needs to have God revealed to him as great, strong, admirable, perfect, all-powerful: the God of the Bible and of Creation, the Lord Jesus and not only, let us repeat, 'Baby Jesus'. Only a God of greatness and strength corresponds completely to the aspirations of a child who is trying to grow.[1]

Acts of religion should stand out for the child by their particular dignity and grandeur and as those amongst his activities which bring him to share most in the life of adults. Everything which concerns God and religion should have something of grandeur about it. A religion which brings everything down to a childish level will have no value for him, but will even interfere with his development by maintaining his childish attitudes instead of helping him outgrow them.

On the contrary, he should be told that God wants to see him grow. The name of the Lord should be associated with everything beautiful, big, exalting, and as little as possible with what is puerile, ugly, bad and dirty. Let us remember God when a good deed is done or when we discover something beautiful, when the child has a particularly happy experience, and not when it is time to scold the child. Instead of saying, 'God sees all the bad things you do', 'God forbids this or that', let us say, 'God sees all the good things you do', 'God loves this or that'.

It should always be remembered that a child is happy to act independently and that grace demands his active collaboration in order to bring fruit. The child should be encouraged to be personal and generous in his religious life, and our behaviour should demonstrate that God loves initiative in religion. If the child gives evidence of spontaneity, if he wants to pray in his own way (on condition that it is respectful), if he asks to visit

---

[1] This does not mean that the Child Jesus does not have a place in the child's religious life. See p. 103.

a church, to offer something to God, to hear a religious story, he should be encouraged, in the very name of God, and helped in achieving his desires. All acts of religion which are done on personal initiative make the child's faith more personal and help him develop in the faith.

THE CHILD TRIES
TO ACT LIKE GROWN-UPS

In his desire to grow, the child looks for a model he can imitate amongst those bigger than he is, expecially amongst adults. The adult represents for him the aim towards which his desire to grow is oriented. Filled with boundless admiration for him and everying he does, the child unconsciously imitates the grown-up in all his words and actions, trying to raise himself to his level, to get some of his glory by imitation.

Among the grown-ups, his parents occupy a special place. Instinctively the child sees them as all-powerful beings who can do anything for him. He watches, admires and tries to imitate them more than all others. If he perceives in them qualities which, although they are far above him, he can understand and imitate in some way—like self-control, calmness, authority—he forces himself to follow in their wake.

It could be supposed that a child who enjoys imitating adults so much could live without inconvenience exclusively in the society of grown-ups. This is not so. For many reasons, he must also mix with other children. A life amongst grown-ups often tires him, and without a friend of his own age he feels lonely and can never feel completely at ease when playing or talking. The presence of other children is useful even for learning to imitate adults : children help one another to discover ways of imitating adults, a certain spirit of competition is set up amongst them which stimulates their initiative. In this way it is easier for them to work towards the satisfaction of their desire to grow.

The presence of brothers and sisters brings with it a multitude of activities in which a child has the opportunity to oppose, assert himself, compare himself and find an audience for his exploits. In their company he learns to discover the reality of others and makes experiments in social living. A child who lives amongst brothers and sisters, even at the cost of frequent clashes, is generally observed to be more sociable than solitary children.

Between brothers and sisters, or between friends, a hierarchy is usually set up, generally based on difference in age. An older child can have greater importance in some respects even than the parents in the life of his brothers and sisters. The presence of a younger child can in return exercise a great influence on the older, either in helping him mature by making him take over the role of a parent or, on the contrary, in keeping him a child longer.

THE CHILD NEEDS AN EXAMPLE WHICH HELPS HIM TO GROW

The first example which presents itself to the child comes from those directly concerned with his education, and their actions should be such as can serve him as models. Actions done well, slowly and calmly, clear and simple statements made with confidence, these he will easily be able to copy. We should not hide our thoughts and feelings if they are within the child's grasp and can contribute to his education. Some of our actions should be accompanied by a commentary, we should 'speak' them as we do them, if this can in the least way be useful in making them more understandable and easier for the child to imitate.

To our own example we should add others, children's as well as grown-ups'. Through pictures, stories, by the account of the lives of other people, by watching those around him, the child will discover the various forms of human activity and enlarge the scope of his experience. We should also let him have the pleasure of having friends of his own age, especially if he has no brothers and sisters of his own.

But it should not be forgotten that the young child imitates without discrimination. We should therefore be watchful of the educative value of what is put before him, and in particular we should take care that there is agreement on this point amongst his educators—that his mother and his teacher have the same idea of education, speak and act in the same spirit and in analogous fashion, that anyone to whom the child is entrusted has the same desire to help him to grow.

LIVING EXAMPLE FOR HIS RELIGIOUS LIFE

At this age the religious life of the child is above all the reflection of that of his environment, for the various reasons we have given : especially because of his imitativeness and his desire to become like a grown-up. To this there is added a supernatural reason : where many Christians are gathered together for the love of God, Jesus is amongst them, uniting them intimately and mysteriously with one another. This consideration is especially valuable for children, who are so easily impressed by the atmosphere around them and who share so intimately the life of the grown-ups they mix with : their faith and religious life especially need the support of those around them. The young child, more than others, needs to have before him the religious example of others in order to model himself on it.

Rather than say, 'Pray like this,' it would be better if we could say, 'Look at how your father (mother, I) prays'—or even better, without our saying anything, he should be allowed to copy our behaviour. We should have it clear in our minds that religious education at this age consists above all in witness and living example. Care should be taken that the way we pray, our deportment before God, our acts of love for God and for our neighbour, while still being worthy of an adult, can yet be imitated in some way by the child.

Not everyone feels at ease in expressing his faith openly. Many suffer from their inability to awaken the religious life of a child. But all have a treasury of living example which the Church puts at their disposal : that of the Bible, the lives of the saints and the Liturgy.

The simplicity of Biblical characters, the spontaneity which they show in their religion, their oriental way of translating their religion into gestures, are especially suited to young children. Moses' gesture of respect before God, of which we have already spoken, his prayer with arms outstretched towards heaven as a sign of supplication, his building of a tent in order to be able to speak with God in silence there : all are examples for the child. Abraham's unquestioning obedience, his readiness to build altars for God, his contemplation of the stars at night, his kindness to his nephew, Lot, can be understood by little children. Samuel's silence and his respectful demeanour before the Lord ('Speak, Lord, for your servant hears you'), King David's beautiful prayers, his way of singing them and of dancing before God, his desire to offer him a beautiful House, the Blessed Virgin praying in her house in Nazareth ('Here is your handmaid, Lord'),[1] the joyful procession of the shepherds towards the Crib, the prostration of the Three Kings before the Child Jesus, Zacchias' hurry to come down from the tree and receive Jesus in his own way into his home . . . all are striking pictures for the child. Some amongst them which seem to be particularly well suited to serve as examples for a certain child should be picked out.[2]

God's own actions in episodes from the Old Testament and the example of Jesus in the Gospels can have great evocative power. But these are no longer the actions of human persons, nor mere examples for the child to imitate. To present them as such to the young child is to risk lowering divine activity to the

---

[1] Whether 'Thou' should be used or 'You' when addressing God is a matter which is best decided by individuals themselves. Whichever comes more naturally is probably the best. However, it should be kept in mind that 'thou' is an unfamiliar pronoun to very young children and it may be advisable to postpone its use until he has had an opportunity to become more familiar with it by hearing it used in church and in school.

[2] Many of these scenes are presented in the year's programme, pp. 127. ff.

level of simple human actions. Here it is more a question of presenting something wondrous for him to contemplate and marvel at.

The spectacle, for example, of certain manifestations of the power and goodness of God, such as the coming down of fire from heaven or of the cloud on the House of God, of God coming to the help of Agar and his little boy in the desert, the spectacle of certain scenes picked from the life of our Lord, could efficaciously help the child to change and to develop : the powerful calmness of Jesus pacifying the stormy waves and reminding the Apostles to be at peace and not afraid will make an impression on him and could help him develop a confidence in Jesus and a way of drawing support from his presence and power which will make him stronger and bigger.[1]

There should also be some examples taken from the life of children. Children love stories which deal with characters like themselves. The Child Jesus of Nazareth in particular has a definite attraction for many.

However, we should not be too eager to turn the child's religion into a demand that he make precise efforts to imitate models. The examples we give should be allowed to work as it were by contagion, communicating to the child a little of the divine glory and influencing his behaviour indirectly. Even the Child Jesus should be presented in this way for, even if Jesus became a child like him and can become his Friend and an irreplaceable example, we should see to it that the child always feels great admiration, respect and true adoration in his regard, as one should for God.[2]

---

[1] Olivier is three and a half years old. He is with an aunt in the mountains when a storm breaks out which makes the house tremble and frightens everyone in it. Olivier is frightened too, but suddenly his aunt sees him kneel down, say a prayer and then get up again declaring, 'I am not frightened any more'. And in fact he was not frightened any longer. Such faith presupposes a real sense of the greatness and the power of God.

[2] On this subject, see the stories on pp. 146, 147.

THE CHILD NEEDS
THE APPROBATION OF ADULTS
IN ORDER TO FEEL BIG

A child can feel that he has reached the level of the grown-ups only if they show him their appreciation. So he is very much concerned to get their approbation.

He shows off and parades himself as something to be admired. The regard and esteem of the adult elate and stimulate him, and confirm in him the feeling of his own value. He wants to please and to merit this esteem and turns incessantly to the adult in the hope of approval.

His joy is at its peak when he sees a grown-up join in doing something with him, or when he is allowed to take part in the activities of an adult.

Let Us Give Him the Support of an Approving Adult

Anyone concerned with a child's education should see to it that he is continually present in the life of the child, as an encouraging witness to his activities. He should know how to show his appreciation of the details of his life by a word here and there and how to satisfy his need for approval with never-ending patience. He should be able to comment with a word of praise (or more rarely, of blame) on the child's activities.

To stimulate him, one should not rely on fear of punishment nor on the hope of rewards, but on the child's desire for esteem and the feeling of satisfaction he has when he has done something well and his actions are approved. Then one will easily be able to turn him into a little helper in the accomplishment of simpler tasks.

The Child Should Come to Know That God is Actively Interested in His Life

It is to his parents and teachers that the child must first of all look for and find approval of his conduct. But his parents must teach him little by little to look beyond them and to turn towards God. This small child, who cannot live without some-one near him to appreciate what he does, should come to know that God does take notice of what he does and is interested in it.

The child should be reminded in the *ordinary course of activity* of God's active attention and, little by little, he should acquire the habit of keeping this in mind. This must be done with discretion, with consideration for the character of each child and without robbing the divine presence of its character of imposing transcendence and mystery. To a child about to do a good deed, one can say with a gesture and expression suggest-ing the nearness of the divine presence, 'The Lord sees you and is pleased'. Through this kind of teaching, the life of certain children of this age can become one of friendship with God or with Jesus, filled with love and religious respect, in the image of those persons in the Bible who 'walked with God'.

Some religious stories, such as those we have mentioned above, and others such as God's choice of the young David to be the one to accomplish great things, God's visit to Elias to comfort him, the attention that Jesus gave to those around him, certain divine interventions in the lives of the saints, as well as the consideration of all the gifts God has made to us in his creation, will convey to a child an idea of the watchful-ness of God over his life and the helping presence of the Lord at his side.

However, the child's activities should not habitually be motivated by the prospect of heavenly reward, even less by the fear of divine punishment, but rather by the feeling that God sees and approves his good actions—and sometimes, with those children who are well balanced psychologically, by the knowledge that God is saddened by what is not good because he cannot approve of it.[1] In telling a child that God rejoices in everything he does well we shall reflect something of God's pleasure and convey with the pride and joy of the saints.

[1] On this delicate point see pp. 118-9.

Over and above this he should be taught that God wants to take him to himself one day, to heaven with the angels and saints : in this way we shall make the child God's ally and raise him in some way to share the glory of God.

THE CHILD IS CAPABLE
OF ACCEPTING RESTRICTIONS FOR
THE SAKE OF ACTING LIKE A GROWN-UP

After a period in which his desire to assert himself takes the form of opposing everything around him, with great tension as a result, the child of three or four usually becomes capable of accepting certain restrictions.

Having rebelled against the demands of his parents and the framework of social customs, he will have discovered by experience that there are some rules to be obeyed, by grown-ups as well as children, some prohibitions which are imposed on everyone, some limits to be respected in the exercise of liberty, which make those who accept them more grown-up. Only 'very small children', 'babies', want to do everything their own way; big people know how to submit to rules. In the light of these discoveries there awakens in the child a sense of order and obligation. Now he begins to understand expressions like 'we must', 'it is time to', and he is usually willing to conform to a certain regulation of his family life.

Even more, in spite of occasional violent assertions of independence, the child for the most part likes to be kept in order, if he is managed with understanding authority, firmly and amicably. He acquires a liking for a certain degree of discipline and derives real satisfaction from keeping within certain limits. Even many games at this age consist of imposing certain rules on himself of his own accord, in overcoming some difficulty, in accepting some fixed system, for the simple joy of feeling strong and dominating things by a personal act of will. By submitting to the rules of social life he has found another way of making himself bigger, of imitating the grown-ups and deserving their approbation.

This in great part explains the child's liking for order and routine. The child likes there to be a definite place for each thing, he wants customs to be respected. He takes pleasure in repeating the same actions, the same words, over and over again : he likes rites, he is attracted by regular rhythms. Sometimes he even goes so far as to become fanatic in his habits.[1]

Through this respect for rules and customs, the child is led to control his behaviour and master himself a little : he becomes capable of demanding occasional physical efforts of himself, sometimes even of repressing some desire or of making a 'sacrifice'.

THE CHILD NEEDS A FRAMEWORK OF RULES AND HABITS

As the child has this regard for rules, it is better educational method, as is well known, to use impersonal phrases, such as, 'people must', 'it is not allowed', 'this is how it is done', 'it is a good thing to . . .', 'it is better to . . .', than to use the imperative and exert one's personal authority. At this age, submission to a rule usually makes a child feel bigger, while obedience to the will of another makes him feel inferior.

We should take advantage of this sense of order to point out with clarity what is allowed to him. We should say to him, 'This is good, this is not good'. Often the best way of counteracting his excessive liveliness is to remind him of the limits within which a child must keep himself if he wants to grow and act like the grown-ups. The most important of these rules is that a child must obey his parents.

In the same way the child should acquire the habit of carrying on his activities within a framework of regular habits : there should be some ritual about going to bed, getting up, having meals . . . carried out at fixed times. We should see to it, however, that this is not so meticulously regulated as to drive

---

[1] His liking for order also comes from a need for security. Order in things and in activities are reassuring to the child and allow him to feel at home and orient himself in his environment with certainty.

the child to obsessiveness and fanaticism but allow some play to his liberty.

Again, this sense of order will help us to teach him to appreciate the things well done and to lead him to respect certain elementary forms of politeness. On the same lines we can teach him to hold himself well and acquire a good posture.

Rhythmical exercises are good to help the child acquire control of his body and learn to move harmoniously. Good muscular training and the learning of certain movements— first those of everyday life—made deliberately and methodically will make self-control easier to achieve. We already saw in the first part that play material which appeals to his imagination, is educative and properly graded, is also very helpful in this.

However, let us remember that this regard for rules and customs, good habits and tidiness and self-control cannot be developed in a child except in a peaceful atmosphere where everything has its place and in the company of adults, who, because they are themselves capable of self-control, can achieve this peace and order around them.

LET US TEACH THE CHILD TO MAKE HIS LIFE MORE PLEASING TO GOD BY IMPOSING CERTAIN DEMANDS ON HIMSELF

A child who has a feeling for the right thing to do, and especially a young Christian in the state of grace understands very well that his dealings with God have to be marked by a special dignity and respect. He will find it fitting that they make greater demands on him than any other activity.

RULES AND   This child who one day will have to learn to obey
HABITS   God's commandments should be required from
                 now on to hold himself properly before God in
prayer : he should know how to stand straight, without moving, with hands joined, how to be silent for a while before his

Lord, and any gestures accompanying his prayers should be done slowly and with devotion.

He could express his adoration, for example, by a great gesture of greeting; his admiration by stretching his arms out on each side; his love by pressing his hands to his heart; his self-offering by lifting his hands up; his joy by throwing his arms upwards. When he is bigger, it will be easier to obey a God whom he is already used to surrounding with such respect from his youth (see below, pp. 115ff.).

It should not be claimed that such gestures are artificial. On the contrary, they are natural for the child of this age. It is the dryness of an adult attitude which is artificial for him. Why not allow each to express himself in his own way in family prayers? The child does not express his affection for his parents in the same way as an older person does. We should not force a stiff and formal attitude into his religious life. We should attune ourselves to him and imitate with faith and sincerity those attitudes of devotion drawn from the example of persons in the Bible and the Liturgy. He should be allowed to reproduce them in his prayer, with respect, *if this can help him to find contact with God*—and there are many whom this does help. School teachers who deal with groups of children of the same age often have fewer difficulties than parents in this respect. The family should see to it that the child's devotions at home profit by the influence of religious practices at school.

A particular part of the house or of the classroom, a corner arranged as a little oratory, can be reserved for devotions. The child should be allowed to go there at will to greet our Lord or the Blessed Virgin, to ask a favour, or to offer something.[1]

Religious activities are more attractive to a child when he

---

[1] In certain families the oratory is even a small separate room, transformed into a sanctuary: Crucifix and Madonna, curtains the colour of the liturgical season serving as background for a picture which changes according to the feasts, pictures of patron saints or religious mementos of the family hanging on the wall (Baptisms, first Communions, parents' marriage, vocations in the family, etc.).

can impose some rules on himself in carrying them out : regularity in prayer in the morning and at night, the custom of a moment's recollection before and after meals, some small ritual observed in prayers or religious conversations. A child likes a regular rhythm in his prayers. A story often repeated becomes an object of special veneration for him.

EFFORT AND SACRIFICE His whole life can be gradually transformed by this desire to behave in a way worthy of God and by the attraction which the example of Jesus will have for him. His religion will thus slowly become a striving towards good. He should be *discreetly* encouraged in this direction, and we should help him by explaining clearly what attitudes, actions, habits, are pleasing to God and can make his life more beautiful. With discretion, and within the limits possible to each, we should suggest, as the occasion presents itself, the kind of behaviour which God expects of him and which will make him bigger.

The child grasps the beauty of an action done for God especially when he has the joy of mastering himself a little for God's sake. Just as Jesus achieved greatness in accepting to suffer courageously and merited as a reward the joy of Easter, the child will feel like a man too and will experience an inner joy if he does something a little difficult for God : if he gives up something that he likes, if he obeys a command or rule that he dislikes, if he holds back some characteristic liveliness or a fit of anger, if he keeps his activity within certain limits.[1]

It would be very clumsy and very harmful to the child to expect him to struggle against himself continuously, especially in the name of God. This is not the age to start the habit of self-sacrifice (without a manifest indication of grace from God). But when a favourable opportunity presents itself, we should be able tactfully to suggest some action which is a little difficult, in imitation of Jesus or some saint.

[1] See the yearly programme on how to present Lent to children of this age.

3

THE CHILD NEEDS A RELIGION WHICH ENGAGES HIS AFFECTIONS

THE THREE- and four-year-old child, driven by his desire to assert himself and conquer the world, makes contact with everything around him. But his enthusiasm for exploring and his desire to grow are not enough to bring about an intimate relationship between him and his environment and to integrate him profoundly with social life. Only the affection which he feels for those around him and the love he receives from them can create this vital relationship, without which the child will be unsociable and, as it were, uprooted all his life.

Parents and teachers should therefore see to it that he is always treated with proper affection. In his religious life we should strive to establish a personal relationship between him and God. We should reveal to him the love which God bears him.

Moreover, this child, apparently so full of self-confidence, is in fact troubled in the deeper recesses of his soul. His relationships with his parents and brothers and sisters can be affected by this worry which comes mainly from the fear of not being loved. Care should be taken to avoid anything which might make him uncertain of our affection. Above all, God must not be presented to him under a menacing aspect. He must always feel that God loves him.

Little by little, as he becomes conscious of others, the child will become capable of acts of kindness springing from his own free will, and we should help him in this. Let us try to orient his religion towards an active love of God and of others.

THE CHILD
NEEDS AFFECTION

At this age, the child manifests his emotional needs more cautiously than before. A certain balance seems to have been established between his needs for affection and his sense of dignity. His mother's affection is no longer his only source of inner satisfaction. But he is still emotionally sensitive and at all ages needs to love and to be loved. Affection is as necessary to him as air and freedom, as words and pictures.

Even friendly companionship is not enough for him any more. Deep within him he experiences the need for a more personal, more complete love. Now there appear signs which give evidence of the beginnings of a new love, of a more jealous and passionate kind. At this age the expression 'I love' takes the place of 'I like', some children speak of 'marrying' one of their parents, there are occasional outbursts of affection for some member of the family circle.

Insufficient or excessive affection at this age often leaves its mark for life and many emotional troubles in adult life have their origins in the frustrations and shocks experienced in this period.

LET US SURROUND THE CHILD WITH AFFECTION

In the interest which his educators take in him, the child should perceive a note of *personal friendship,* as well as their esteem and approbation. If he meets with this friendship, the child, who has such an exalted conception of the adult, will be fully satisfied. He and the adult will begin a shared life and an understanding which will create a bond of exceptional strength and make a sociable being of the child, often for life.

We must see to it, therefore, that this young child finds around him the atmosphere of warm affection necessary for his development : amongst brothers and sisters and friends of his own age and, if possible, friendly teachers and above all affectionate parents.

The presence of brothers and sisters in a united family, or friends in a class where there is a spirit of harmony, gives the child opportunity for numerous emotional satisfactions and contributes to an atmosphere in which he can blossom out. It should be realized that children in their relationships with each other most often imitate the behaviour of the adults of their environment among themselves or towards the children.

Educators other than parents should show their affection discreetly, above all by a friendly manner, welcoming, attentive, encouraging at the same time. A child's life is gladdened by friendliness on the part of adults.

Of parents more is expected. Without letting themselves become excessively affectionate on every possible occasion, which would spoil the child's progress and would come to thwart his need to grow, they should not forget his secret desire for love. No day should pass without their giving some evidence of their affection and they should welcome any demonstration of affection on his part. Their relationship should have a certain note of intimacy : mother, for example, can confide little secrets to her child—an excellent method of making him feel sure of being especially loved. Nor should the father feel excused from this duty. The child must feel that he has in his parents two loving friends and that he will always find in them confidants ready to listen to him sympathetically.

The child also needs to feel that there exists perfect harmony between his parents. Any emotional discord troubles the child deeply. He is as one with his parents and their disunity is insupportable for him because it divides him within himself, plunges him into uncertainty and anguish. He needs to feel the love of his father and his mother and to feel that between them there exists the same love with which he is loved. Only then will he feel the unity of the family and experience the deep and reassuring joy of having the unfailing support of a strong and certain love, the same in each of his parents.

WE MUST REVEAL TO THE CHILD GOD'S LOVE FOR HIM

If our teaching of religion does not aim at revealing the love of God to this little baptized child, it will be seriously misleading and unable to satisfy his deeper longings. He will not be wholly captivated and his religion will run the risk of being no more than empty adoration with no heart behind it. Whenever he hears God mentioned, the child should feel love.

A PERSONAL AND TENDER LOVE — A living bond of love cannot be formed between the child and his God unless the child feels himself personally loved by God.

God's particular love for him can be pointed out in the events that happen to him, through his joys in the family and at school and, above all, by surrounding him with genuine love ourselves, in the image of the love which God bears him. Thus the child's respect for God will be mixed with a certain affection. Expressions like 'my God', 'my Jesus' may come spontaneously with exterior signs of affection. How can love grow if it cannot be freely expressed? There is no reason to exclude such manifestations of emotion towards God, provided that we ourselves use them only with discretion before the child and that they are always accompanied by genuine adoration on our part.

We should not think, however, that the better to speak of divine love we should insist less on the majesty of God. Majesty and love, far from being opposites, reinforce each other in the child's mind. If the child has a very high idea of God, he will be all the more deeply affected to learn that this Lord is full of goodwill towards him, that he looks on him with friendship and is interested in his actions. The more the child is

impressed by God's majesty, the more he will be sensitive to
the marks of his love.

This love and majesty can be pointed out particularly in the
loving care which God showed the people of the Old Testament, in the spectacle of creation, in scenes from the life of
our Lord, in the maternal image of the Blessed Virgin, in the
presence of angels and in certain episodes in the lives of saints.

IN THE OLD   There is no need to omit the Old Testament
TESTAMENT   from the religious education of the young child,
              as some educators believe; on the contrary,
faithful to the spirit of the Church and fitting in with the child's
natural and supernatural needs, we can present him the Old
Testament in the light of the Gospel.[1] When relating some story
from the Old Testament it is best always to emphasize the love
of God which it reveals, even more explicitly than the literal
text of the story itself. For example, in the story of the Burning
Bush, besides the mysterious majesty of the invisible God let
us convey to the child all the love of a God who comes to the
help of his friend and his people. When God let hail come down
from heaven, it is to help Moses and to save his friends. From
any religious story, the child should draw, besides the intuition
of God's majesty, the feeling that he is a very loving Father,
who loves him personally more than the best of Fathers.

IN CREATION The same conviction should develop through
             the discovery of creation. When the child
prays, let us always add a note of personal love to admiration
and praise of God for the wonders of nature. It is to God that
children owe their body, with which they can do so many
good things.

Let us also point out to these little ones the law of love which
is put by the Lord in all of nature and which is at the root
of its fertility ('Go forth and multiply' says God, now as always,

---

[1] On this 'Christian revelation' of the Old Testament, see Appendix I:
Justification of the Biblical Approach.

to all his living creatures, Genesis I). The observation of
plants or animals (an aquarium, for example) can allow him
to make this discovery concretely. Children who find an
atmosphere of real affection at home can be made to thank
God for the joy of having a mother and a father and, if such
is the case, brothers and sisters. They will acquire the habit of
knowing how to give or share what they have received.

THE GOODNESS OF   As much and even more than by the
THE LORD JESUS   wonders of creation, the love of God will
                 be emphasized by the person of Jesus,
radiating majesty and goodness, at once so human and so
divine, and by the words he spoke.

The majesty, the glory and the presence of angels which
underline the greatness of the mystery of Christmas should not
hide but, on the contrary, should make more attractive to them
the *love* of the Child-God come for their sakes from heaven to
the lowly Crib, in a form so accessible to little children. The
life of this young Lord in Nazareth will show him to be very
near their life. The 'Master' surrounded by so much respect
on the part of great and small during his public life and so
great in everything he does must also appear to them marvellously good : he welcomes everyone, helping the unfortunate
and those who are in pain, he speaks to them of the goodness
of the Father in heaven, of the law of love, he lets little ones
whom he especially loves come to him freely.[1]

The sight of the Cross, with the contrast that it offers
between the majesty of him who suffers and the spectacle of
his suffering, accepted for love of us, can bind the child's heart
to Jesus for life. The return of the resurrected Christ to be
with his friends, his ascension into heaven in glory, which
should be made to seem not an absence but a means for Jesus
to prepare a place near God for him, the active friendship
which he continues to show from heaven to the apostles and
all his friends on earth, his presence in the Tabernacle, his

[1] See below, the story of Jesus and the children, pp. 147-8.

loving presence in priests, in parents, in the Christian teachers around him, will succeed in gaining the heart of the child.[1]

We must somehow make this love and this presence of God, this friendship with our Lord, tangible, and present to the child. If he asks, 'Where is Jesus?' we should answer with respect and awe, 'The Lord Jesus is in heaven', but we should add immediately in a more intimate and joyful tone, 'But he is also with us, because we are his friends'.

We can speak of the presence of Jesus with the child, near the child, but not yet of his presence in the child. This is an outward-going age when the child is not yet sufficienctly aware of what goes on within him, and mention of the presence of God within him runs the risk of remaining no more than words for him and of being accompanied by images of physical localization, damaging for his faith. Gradually, as he matures, his relationship with God will deepen and awaken an interior echo in him. Normally it is only towards the age of five or six, and then only if they have been gradually led to it, that children who are living in a Christian atmosphere can profitably learn that God is present within them. Earlier than this, it is not advisable except in special cases of children who are naturally or supernaturally precocious.

The presence of Jesus in the Tabernacle draws many young Christians, for it is the sign of the nearness of the love of their Lord and Friend; but such young children can learn more about this great mystery through the adult's attitude than by explanations.

THE BLESSED VIRGIN   The Blessed Virgin should, with Jesus, play a part in the child's religion, no matter how young he is. Her presence puts a note of

---

[1] Have those who advise against speaking of the life of Jesus to the small child realized the inestimable religious treasure which a certain familiarity, acquired at an early age, even before the age of reason, can mean to the Christian for his whole life? It is evidently necessary that there should be an atmosphere of real faith and that the adult himself really feel love and adoration for our Lord and believe in the educative and supernatural value of the mysteries of his life for the children's souls.

maternal tenderness in his religion which is most satisfying to him. However, she should not be presented to him at this age as his own mother. He will mistakenly conclude that he has two mothers, and will run the risk of unconsciously identifying his earthly mother with the Virgin Mary, which could somewhat alter, for life perhaps, the religious character of his love for the Blessed Virgin. We should speak of her, at this age, as the 'Mother of the Lord Jesus'.

ANGELS AND   Angels and saints should also be spoken of, but
SAINTS   with discretion. Mention of them awakens
                  wonder in the child, for, in their way, they demonstrate the greatness of God and his love. The knowledge of their existence is at once appealing and reassuring to him.

THE CHILD CANNOT BEAR
THE IDEA OF NOT BEING LOVED

The child's secret and deep-rooted need for love is sometimes the cause of serious troubles. Jealousy is always just below the surface and can lead the child to violence. This for the most part unconscious hostility towards people dear to him—parents, brothers, sisters—can in its turn cause hidden feelings of guilt. In certain children anxiety results, on the lower level of consciousness, and manifests itself in dreams full of disturbing images, in angry words or deeds or in involuntary deviations of character or behaviour. Even without such extremes, the onset of open rivalry often indicates the presence of jealousy.

These emotional troubles appear most markedly, though not exclusively, in 'unloved' children, who are living in an atmosphere of family discord, or when there is a marked change in family circumstances, as for example the birth of a younger child who suddenly absorbs the whole attention of the family. If this anxiety is not pacified the moment it appears, conflicts and compensatory activities will develop in the child and hinder his development; even serious psychic disorders, which may weigh heavily on all his future may result. Such cases are unfortunately not rare.

At the root of these troubles is nearly always to be found the child's absolute and fundamental need to be loved for himself. At this age a child can only painfully share the love of those around him with others. Just as he cannot bear to see someone asserting himself in his presence without trying to assert himself in a similar way (otherwise he will experience intolerable feelings of inferiority), so he cannot bear to see anyone receive some mark of affection from his parents if he himself seems to be excluded from it : he feels robbed of a love which is due to him, and has the intolerable impression that he is no longer loved.

Everything Should Be Avoided Which Might Make the Child Feel Unloved

We should beware of anything, therefore, which might give the child the impression that he is not loved, or is loved less than others, that he is abandoned, even if only for a short time, by his family, that he is cut off from them, somehow separated from their affection.

Phrases like, 'You are a lot of trouble to me', 'I am angry with you', 'Daddy will punish you when he comes', should be avoided, especially with sensitive children. Our reproaches should not appear to be a withdrawal of love. Phrases like, 'I am going to give you away to somebody', 'A policeman will come and take you away', etc., should never be used.

It should be realized that a threat at this age is interpreted by the child as a possible banishment from love, or as a desire to make him feel inferior, in other words, as nastiness on the part of the adult. Such a procedure, far from bettering his inward disposition, usually incites him to be nasty himself, either by imitation or by reaction.

Generally speaking, anything which might make him jealous should be avoided : comparisons between brothers and sisters, obvious unfairness, marked favouritism.

If it is necessary to reprimand a child (or if we want to stimulate him in some way) it is better to appeal to his need for esteem than to his desire for affection. Otherwise the child who cannot respond to our appeal will feel guilty with respect to the love he owes us and could feel cut off from our affection, of which he has an absolute need. It is preferable to make objective remarks, pointing out the wrongness of his attitude, the unfairness it causes, the troubles which his behaviour brings for him and for others. We can say to him, 'That's not good', 'You are going to hurt your little brother', 'You are upsetting your father's work', 'A child who makes too much noise (òr something else) can't stay in this room', 'A child who doesn't eat his soup doesn't get any pudding'. It should not be forgotten, however, that a child also needs to feel esteemed and such reproaches should not be multiplied indefinitely, nor should we ever say, for example, 'You are good for nothing', 'You will never amount to anything'.

In the same way, if punishment becomes necessary, it should not be done in a way which will affect him emotionally; the child should not be left with the impression that he is not wanted or that he is despised. After being reprimanded, he should be able to take up his activities again knowing that he is loved and capable of doing well.

Parents should make it their special task to understand what is going on in the mind of their child, especially when he is going through a difficult period. They should help him to get rid of his fears if this is necessary. In periods of anxiety he needs reassurance and has to feel that he is surrounded by special love. We should not forget the importance of moments of greater intimacy to resolve an interior crisis. It should be remembered that a nightmare which involves the idea of struggle or chase by a nasty animal often betrays anxiety of an emotional kind.

Some stories can help to free the child from his fears. On this question, it is not necessary to insist on the principle that all mention of nasty animals and fearful events is to be absolutely avoided. Actually the best method to free the child from a fear is to bring it occasionally to his mind, to let him relive it in a symbolic form through some story which may at first frighten him. Then one can strive to counteract the feeling of fear by bringing the story skilfully to a happy conclusion which frees the child entirely from this fear. The end of the story should leave the child feeling quite at peace. If he has really 'followed' the story he will have passed from anxiety to calmness and have overcome his fear. Stories like Tom Thumb, Snow White and many other fairy tales can achieve this result. But to do this successfully, it is necessary to know how to gauge their effect, and stories of this kind are not equally suited to all children.

THE CHILD SHOULD FEEL SURE THAT HE IS ALWAYS LOVED BY GOD

The fear that his heavenly Father or Jesus no longer loves him will be as disastrous for the child of this age as it is offensive to God's goodness. It would be most ill-advised, then, to have the child associate the name of God with fear, punishment, or even threats.

Phrases like, 'If you do this, God will punish you', 'God has punished you', 'God is angry with you', 'Jesus does not love you any more' should be avoided all together. The child should not be haunted by the idea that God is angry with him. His religion should be one of love : it is not fear that should inspire his desire for good and his efforts, but love of God and of Jesus, and a sense of awe and great respect.

The child of this age should not be presented those scenes from the Bible where God intervenes to punish, as in the story of Cain, the Flood, the destruction of Sodom and Gomorrha, the threat to Niniveh, the judgment of the damned. Frightening pictures should be discarded : for example Abraham brandishing a knife over his son, the judgment of Solomon, the martyrdom of the seven Maccabees, and above all, pictures of hell and the devil.

The usual way of presenting Bible stories and illustrating them seems to aim mainly at inspiring fear in a child; but these stories have other possibilities. As we have already mentioned, it is possible by a careful choice of words and details, without distorting the facts and without robbing them of their grandeur, to make the love which God has put into them stand out. The first way is dangerous with young children and ends with the perversion of religious feeling : the child is then either tempted to liberate himself from the fearful presence of such a merciless God, or else begins the anguish of feeling guilty, condemned by God and rejected by him. Only the way of love is proper for young Christians, and most especially is this true before the age of reason.

The child needs to know that no matter what happens, he is always loved by God. He must always feel sure of finding a welcome and a personal love for himself in him. There must never be question, therefore, of connecting any of his actions with 'sin' and certainly not with 'hell'. Nor should we speak of God in connection with his jealousies : God does not condemn suffering, he pities it and asks us to relieve it. Our manner of speaking of God should bring the child the profound, unalterable peace he needs.

THE CHILD IS CAPABLE OF ACTS
OF GOODWILL TOWARDS OTHERS

At the age of two, at his mother's suggestion and out of affection for her, the child is capable of little acts of renunciation for someone he knows, his father for example.[1] It is an age when he can acquire habits of helpfulness and active goodwill. At the age of three and four, it is quite a different story !

With the assertion of his personal will, the child discovers the difference between 'mine' and 'yours', he acquires a sense

---

[1] Bruno is two and a half. His mother offers him a sweet. He takes it and runs to give it to his father, with obvious pleasure. Only after this does he come to get one for himself, although he likes sweets very much.

of property : to give something to someone is to deprive oneself of that thing. Also, at the age of three, the child often passes through an individualistic period of furious egocentricity. However, the evolution of his emotional life will lead him gradually to a new and different awareness of others and make him capable of acts of goodwill again, this time more personal and under his control. This is how the change takes place.

When the child of three or four discovers that his mother, or some other person particularly dear to him, loves persons other than him, he is invariably tempted to jealousy, and he is seized by the desire to re-establish the bond of emotional identity which tied him to her in his infancy. But everyday experience forces him to notice the facts : he and his mother are two distinct beings.

Gradually, he learns to think of her as distinct from him and to separate himself from her. His mother becomes a personality opposing his, a desirable personality whom he tries to dominate. To achieve this, the child becomes capable of giving up his personal desires and of yielding to the wishes of someone he loves.

Thus the same love drives him, on the one hand, to keep his mother only for himself, to be tyrannical about her and, on the other hand to submit to her, to become her obliging servant, to make himself worthy of love in her eyes. An attachment, egocentric in its origin, gradually puts the child on his way to the discovery of others and towards an active love.

The child of four progressively extends this discovery to include other people around him. He realizes little by little that his friends also have an existence separate from his, a family of their own, a father, a mother, personal troubles and personal feelings.

This insight into the lives of others is intermittent, however, and does not prevent him from being normally self-centred and a stranger to the rest of the world; but it can make him capable of momentary acts of goodwill and of true sensitivity. So it happens that a child gives in to someone else, collaborates with him for an instant, helps, shares, lends his things.

The child should be encouraged to love others. With discretion and as far as the child can respond to it with some joy, let us appeal to his feelings to lead him to acts of detachment and generosity towards his parents and teachers, his brothers and sisters, his playmates and the other persons around him.

In all these cases, a certain compensation is necessary to him : we should show him our appreciation, pointing out the pleasure he is causing and the help he is giving; but we should not react to his generosity with excessive effusions of affection, which would have the effect of turning the child back on himself in a self-centred and self-satisfied way reminiscent of his earlier childhood; we should now be helping him to grow up and encouraging his progress towards unselfishness.

The example of our own readiness to help, our own patience towards more difficult children and our attentive care for each one is one of the most efficacious means of leading the child to the love of others. We should try to include him in whatever we do in this direction and help him identify himself with our feelings. We should help him discover the joy he can give others by his thoughtfulness. In this way anything which will develop his considerateness for others should be encouraged : looking after a younger child, taking part in a common task.

Thus he will come to like doing certain things which up to this time he had regarded merely as opportunities for showing his superiority. He will begin to feel friendship for those around him. He will develop and not live turned back on himself. This is a particularly good way of preventing feelings of solitude, or of overcoming some secret jealousy.

THE CHILD'S RELIGION SHOULD BE ORIENTED TOWARDS AN ACTIVE LOVE OF GOD AND OTHERS

Through the example of the charity of his teachers, the child's religion should gradually be transformed into an active search for what can please God and others.

Witness and living example are still the best method of teaching here. Practical suggestions made to the child at the right moment will help him to pass on to actions. Episodes from the Old Testament, the Gospels and (with prudence) from the lives of the Saints, presented in the spirit we have described, and the beauty of the works of creation can also provide the child with incentive to please.

When he sees the love with which a God so great looks down on him, the solicitude which Jesus showed in the mysteries of his life and with which he still surrounds him now, the way in which some of God's friends responded to this love, the child will spontaneously come to want to please God and Jesus. It will then become possible to orient the child towards the religious search for good, not only through his desire to grow up, but through his love of God as well.

Let us choose as examples of love of God and one's neighbour acts which are within the child's scope. Let us particularly emphasize in the episodes from the Gospels which we tell him all the acts of goodness which Jesus did. We should show him Jesus extending his hands over the sick to comfort them and cure them, consoling those who wept, forgiving those who had done wrong : one day, so that a mother would no longer weep, he took the hand of her dead son and gave him back to her full of life; another day, some people wanted to throw stones at a woman and Jesus stopped them; another time, to show that we should be good to everyone, Jesus told the story of the Good Samaritan.[1] Pictures of these scenes, practical activities which should be carried out when these stories are told, will help the child to keep the feelings of love alive.

The example of Jesus, especially in the crib and on the Cross, will entice the child to do good acts. We can then carefully suggest some act of kindness for God towards a little brother or sister or friend, some service cheerfully done for parents or teacher. The motives for these acts of charity will doubtless be

---

[1] See pp. 150-1 for this story. A story told by Jesus has more value for a Christian child than one which has simply been invented.

mixed, but the grace of God which is in his soul will find a way and will enliven with real charity some of his efforts to imitate Jesus.

THE NEED FOR PRAYER ON THE PART OF THOSE EDUCATING A CHILD

One of the primary conclusions to be drawn from this portrait of the child of three and four and the advice accompanying it—a conclusion which is confirmed in practice—is that the religious life of the child at this age is largely a reflection of that of his immediate environment. The responsibility of parents and teachers in the child's spiritual formation is very great.

However, the primary and true cause of the child's spiritual progress is neither his parents nor his teachers nor his environment but God. The influence of human environment is necessary, but it is only a condition. Only God can cause and develop true faith and charity—that is, a supernatural life—in the human soul. No man, no matter how holy, can give the faith to a child by his mere influence. A teacher sows by word and example—God causes the divine seed to grow.

It is not enough, therefore, to adapt oneself to the child's psychology or even to give him example : it is also necessary to pray, and pray a great deal, for him. It is here that the duty of a Christian educator begins and ends : to pray to God to enlighten the child and touch his heart, to pray to the Holy Spirit to carry out his divine work in the child in spite of our clumsy efforts and our insufficiencies. With this we should begin and end each of our days. Fortunately this is something we are all capable of doing.

So we should feel both humble and confident. God's grace can triumph over all obstacles, it can make good the unfortunate results of our gropings. However, we should not forget that our duty to pray has not only the good of the child as its object, but also our own, on which the good of the child depends so much. Let us pray humbly to God to help us perfect our skill as educators but, even more, to increase our faith and charity so that in our company the child may develop and like Jesus advance 'in wisdom with the years, and in favour with God and with men'.

PART TWO

THE RELIGIOUS LIFE OF THE CHILD
IN GREATER DETAIL

OUTLINE

AT THE end of this exploration of the development and education of the three- and four-year-old child, the reader may find
it hard to separate the general themes from the many details.
So, in this section of the book, we shall first briefly sum up the
advice on religious education contained in Part One, in
order to formulate its *general laws*. Then, we shall go on to
apply these laws to certain essential *religious themes*.

1 GENERAL LAWS RELATING TO THE RELIGIOUS FORMATION OF THE CHILD

THE FUNDAMENTAL CONDITION—A FAVOURABLE ENVIRONMENT

THE RELIGIOUS education of a baptized child presupposes as a basic condition the living faith of those teaching him.

Only a living witness can reveal to a young Christian the living God of his Baptism, and make God's majesty and love effectively present to him. Without this faith on an educator's part there will normally be no contact between the child and God, there will be no religious life.

It is the faith of those around him which allows the seed of faith received at Baptism to grow and which gives religious value to the techniques used in his education, whatever these may be. This is truly the fundamental condition.

To be really effective, however, this faith needs the help of a suitable environment and atmosphere, which, moreover, will themselves be the natural result of this faith.

In his normal environment at home and at school, the child should find first of all love, respect for his nascent dignity, an authority which commands respect, calmness and joy.

If he is not loved, the child will never discover the love of God. If he himself is not the object of a certain respect, how will he ever come to realize his own dignity as a child of God?

If he does not meet with anyone strong and firm who knows
how to make certain demands of him and resist him, it will be
difficult for him to come to perceive anything of the majesty
of God or ever to learn to submit to the divine will. Without
calmness, he cannot become attentive to the presence of God.
Without joy, he will have little spiritual drive.

Within this environment, the child needs a religious atmosphere as well, in order to develop his supernatural life. And
the four elements essential to such an atmosphere cannot be
repeated too often : first of all silence, which should surround
the child's religious activities like a rampart, an indispensable
condition for a personal contact of some depth with God;
special respect for anything which has to do with God, which
alone can reveal the divine transcendence and the sacred
character of religion; the religious transparency of those teaching him, who should have the simplicity to live their religious
life openly before him, letting their faith and love of God shine
through their words, their expression, their attitude; finally,
divine joy and peace in which all spiritual activity should be
bathed and which will be tangible signs of the love of God.

The Three Aspects of His Religion

MAJESTY   Since the ages of three and four are characterized
            by the child's desire to grow and to assert him-
self, the first characteristic which should strike him in his
religion is its grandeur and majesty. God should be presented
to him as the God of greatness. Everything should conspire to
give him this impression from the very beginning—not only the
atmosphere of silence, but the tone of voice, the way of standing, the seriousness of his teacher's attitude and of all religious
proceedings. The use of religious language, the retelling of
biblical scenes which emphasize the divine transcendence and
the discovery of creation by the child will also make a very
effective contribution here.

LOVE   Another of the child's traits, more secret but nevertheless fundamental, is his need for love. When we speak
to him of God's majesty, we must always indivisibly associate
with it his goodness, and even more than this, his personal love
for the child. Goodness and majesty, love and power, far from
contradicting each other, reinforce each other in the eyes of a
small child.

Besides the spiritual joy of those teaching him, the principal
means of making him conscious of divine goodwill will be their
discreet and natural association of God with everything which
is a source of joy for the child, particularly the happy events
of his life, the spectacle of nature, the discovery of personal
gifts which God has given him (riches of body and mind, the
happiness of having parents, home and family) and above all
the love which his parents themselves will show him. So also
will Bible stories and lives of the saints which show God's goodness towards men and, particularly, active contemplation of
certain scenes in the life of Jesus. Readings and scenes will
come alive for him through our faith, and should lead him
little by little to turn spontaneously to God in the course of his
life.

WONDER AT   The third essential trait of the child's soul is
THE ABSOLUTE   his need for wonder and the absolute, springing from his thirst for grandeur, his inner
vitality, the creative and magic powers of his imagination and
the absolute character of his thought—all these characteristics
being transformed by his supernatural need for God. If the
name of God and religion are associated with actions, events,
impressions, which just because they are absolutely genuine,
exalt and awe the child by their association with grandeur, love,
vitality and transcendence, then God will appear to him not
only as someone real and great who loves him, but at the same
time as someone who delights his soul, who answers to the
deepest longings of his nature and his life of grace : he will
truly be the God he needs.

This awe of God and religion can be developed by associating in the child's mind the presence and thought of God with everything which is life, power, greatness, transcendence, love, joy, beauty, light. But carefully! Let us take care that God, truly existing and really so wonderful, and the whole supernatural world surrounding him, is put by the child in the domain of the 'real', clearly distinguished from merely imaginary, magic 'wonders'.

METHODS

Actions, words, pictures, living example : these are the means of communication which answer his mental need, for at this age the child must start from what he sees and hears.

AN ACTIVE RELIGION   It is above all by gestures and attitudes, by activities and personal actions done for God that the child can discover God's existence and his presence near him and can begin to have a personal relationship with him. Through action the child's attention is effectively fixed and his thought can concentrate on God. The religion of a small child must be 'acted out' and active. For religious gestures and the actions which he should be taught to make, it is useful to draw inspiration above all from the Bible and the Liturgy.

A SPOKEN RELIGION   Together with action, words are the principal means by which a child of this age discovers and dominates. He must be able to 'talk' and 'sing' his religion in order to enter naturally into the world of religion, or he will run the risk of living there as a stranger. He needs to know the language of religion as well as the technique of silence.

The child of this age does not expect explanations from us, but rather the simple formulation of certain religious truths which are accessible to him, the affirmation of essential truths of faith which he can make his own, the expression of religious

ideas within his reach in the form of prayers for example. The
simplicity of the ideas, the clarity and seriousness of the
language, their adaptation to the child's mind are not enough
to make the supernatural real to him. A formulation which is
truly religious is necessary as well, and this is to be found in
the Church, which has preserved for us in the Scriptures and
the Liturgy the way, inspired by the Lord himself, to speak of
God and to pray.

To this let us add a perfect loyalty to the child : let us never
present to him as true, especially in the course of his religious
education, those things which are only fantasies or legends, or
even those which are not certainly authentic (see pp. 52ff.).

A RELIGION WHICH MAKES   Whether one likes it or not, the
USE OF PICTURES   child lives in a world of mental
                          images. He can think only
through pictures. Starting from them he builds his own particular universe, different from ours, which is coloured by his
imaginings. It is important that he be given the means of
representing to himself the world of religion through images
which do not betray both its real and its supernatural character.

This is to include not only the drawings, paintings and sculp-
tures which he sees, but also any particular thing around him
which presents itself to the child and can be associated by him,
however distantly, with the supernatural, everything which
his imagination can get hold of to people his religious world.

Let us be particularly careful not to give God a material
image. We should start from pictures which can somehow convey the idea of divinity : pictures of God's works of creation,
his manifestations in the course of history, the attitudes of people
in the Bible, the priest's gestures in the liturgy (which we can
perform for him). But it is the religious life of those around
which will have a place of priority amongst the 'reality-images'
presented to him.

To have a religious value, these images, whatever they are,
should convey of their own accord something of the grandeur,

love and marvellous richness of life which is in God. The end
to be achieved should always be kept in mind in the method of
presentation, which is not to excite the senses, but by means
of the senses to put the child, through faith, into contact with
God and the supernatural world—a world quite different from
the profane world, but also quite different from an unreal and
purely imaginary world.

A RELIGION BASED ON   This child, in everything he does,
LIVING EXAMPLES   unconsciously mimes everything he
  sees done around him. It is by active
identification with those around him that he learns to know
them and enriches himself through their larger experience. No
other single thing satisfies his desire to grow so much as imitating adults. A good way of educating the child in religion is to
suggest to him, or rather to point out to him, the example of
living models with whom he can identify himself. In this imitation, his love for action, for words and for images are all
satisfied at the same time.

Those in charge of him should try to be amongst the first
of these religious models, but examples should be drawn
from the religious life of others as well, particularly of
persons in the Bible and of the saints. In this way the child will
be able to enrich his religious life. Let us never forget our
objective, which is not to capture the child's imagination nor to
give fuel to his vitality, but to help to establish between him
and God a real relationship and contact and to develop in the
child a genuine religious life.

PRECAUTIONS TO BE TAKEN—VARIOUS STARTING POINTS

These techniques should be used with great prudence. Some
very accomplished teachers hesitate to use them for fear of pro-
faning religion. Gestures quickly become gesticulation, words
mere verbalism, pictures turn into magic symbols, the imitation of religious persons becomes a way of showing off and
play-acting!

However, these methods *are* valuable and, used with faith and discernment, they do help the child to come to God. The Church has always made use of them : liturgical gestures, processions, pictures, stories. . . . Let us draw inspiration from its ways. Let us know above all how to create the same atmosphere as she does around these things : an atmosphere of silence, respect, mystery, living faith, supernatural joy. Then everything will take on a supernatural character for the child.[1]

It remains to enumerate suitable points of departure.

The first starting point is, without doubt, *the religious life of the people around him.* By that we mean :

—in the first place, the example of prayer and Christian life of the adults around him;

—the celebration of the big feasts, in the family or in the class, with their preparation and external display;

—the little occasional lessons in faith, the explanations given by those around him;

—religious readings, given with faith;

—illustrated religious books, chosen with care, commented on with faith, used with discretion and caution, which the child finds around him;

—liturgical ceremonies at which the child may be present;

—and finally, any signs of religious life which the child meets with : material ones like the crucifix, statues, images, little oratory or altar, churches (especially those in his parish), stations of the cross; living symbols, like priests and religious and the Christians in his environment.

Another starting point important for his religious education is *nature,* which serves as the normal and definite frame for his existence and which is full of attraction for him with its natural riches, plants and, above all, animals.

[1] In this way can the radical conflict be resolved which some educationists, with astounding assurance, seem to find between faith on the one hand and techniques on the other (stories and pictures especially) which God in the Old Testament, Jesus in the Gospels, the Church in the Liturgy and many saints have used to awaken and develop faith in the hearts of men, and which the great masters of the spiritual life have used extensively, without ignoring its dangers.

Finally we can start from the *life of the child itself* : from his ordinary everyday life, from events in the family and at school. A bond should be established between all the joys of daily life and him who through them shows his paternal love.

2 RELIGIOUS THEMES

A GOD WHO IS GREAT AND GOOD AND
WATCHES OVER THE CHILD HE LOVES

THE CHILD of three and four cannot grasp ideas in abstract form nor go so far as to have a notion of spirit and it is not possible for him to come to know God through explanations or ordinary stories. It is through examples that he will gain impressions which will help him gradually become conscious of the presence of God.

The kind of examples which are suitable for a child have already been discussed.[1] But the principle factor is the living faith and attitude of whoever is praying with the child or speaking to him, and the religious quality of his stories: through these the child will sense the presence of someone great and good watching over him.

At this age, the child has a need of someone to watch over him, to be interested in him, to love him and help him to develop; the greater the person taking an interest in him, the greater will be the joy and peace he experiences in being loved. It follows that God must not be presented to him in puerile trappings and as part of a childish world, but as a great and wonderful being: the God of Revelation and Creation, the Lord of Heaven and earth, full of majesty, who comes to us in

[1] See mainly pp. 47-50.

order to help us, a God of wonders, who is the source of all
that life and joy which the child sees reflected around him in
nature and feels within himself. The more a child comes to
know about God's majesty, the more he will marvel at his love
when he sees that this God acts towards him like an affectionate father.[1]

To be 'God's friend' like the people in the Bible and the
saints is for the child a thought which will delight him and at
the same time urge him on to do more and more to merit the
love and approval of his Lord.[2]

THE LORD JESUS[3]

His Great Friend Come From Heaven, Full of Majesty and Goodness

At this age it is impossible to explain the distinction of per-

---

[1] With children from families which are not particularly religious or united, it
is only with care and with a certain preparation that the name 'Father'
should be applied to God. Otherwise this word, which is so expressive in
itself and was recommended by Jesus, will not convey God's transcendence
and perfection to the child. After all, the paternal aspect of God was revealed
long after the aspect of God as the 'Lord', and the Jews were first thoroughly
imbued with the idea of the majesty of God; on the other hand, not all
children have a happy attitude to their father and for some the word may well
be associated with painful emotional conflicts. When we speak of God as the
'Heavenly Father', we should be sure that the children grasp the idea of a
perfect or ideal Father.

[2] The expression 'friend of God' is to be understood in the various senses of the
word 'friend': first of all in the passive sense, of someone who is loved by
God, who is always by his side, watching over him and helping him ('The
Lord is with you', 'The Lord is by his child'); and in the active sense, too,
of someone who loves God and shows it by actions worthy of a friend of
God's.

[3] In the pages which follow, we are writing for the children of religious families.
For them, as we have said, early contact with the life of Jesus under the
requisite conditions can be the source of inestimable treasures. We do not
claim, however, that all the ideas we develop must be presented to all
children. We give here a simple explanation, suited to this age, of the
principal mysteries of the life of Jesus in case there should be the need to
speak of them, either because the child is going to take part in some family
celebration of a certain feast or because he wants some explanation of
pictures which he sees around him, or because it is judged useful to his
spiritual life to make these mysteries known and familiar to him. With
children of non-religious background, more restraint must be shown.

sons in God, or to use terms like 'God the Father' and 'God the Son', which will inevitably cause the child to form an idea of two Gods. But it is important in practice to distinguish in the use we make of the words 'God' and 'Jesus', otherwise a confusion will arise in the child's mind which may disturb him for the rest of his life. Now is the time to plant the seed of a distinction which will become clear to him only in the future. Let us call Jesus 'the Son of God', and speak of him as 'Jesus' or 'the Lord Jesus' when we are speaking of something done by God incarnate; let us say 'God' or 'the Lord' in all other cases, especially when it is question of a work of creation or divine intervention in the Old Testament.

As the example of a grown person is more impressive than that of a child, let Jesus the man be presented to him as well as, or even instead of, Jesus the child. We should avoid the mistake, educationally most inadvisable, of using the expression 'baby Jesus' on all occasions, even when speaking of the Lord's public life, his Cross, the Tabernacle or the God of creation. This expression is fittingly used only for the childhood of Jesus and even then, the expression 'the Child Jesus' is preferable, because it is more religious, nearer to the Scriptures and has the advantage that it can be pronounced in a tone of respect.

Without doubt, a child, especially a Christian child, is attracted to the Child Jesus in the Crib and at Nazareth and will be moved at seeing the Crib or hearing about him. In such an attraction the workings of grace may be present. But is this not, within limits, something similar to the attraction he feels in ordinary life to babies in the family and towards friends of his own age? The affection that he feels for these babies and friends, which corresponds to a real need, is different and complementary to what he feels for his parents and teachers. Each kind of affection is good in its own way.

It is true that he finds in the Child Jesus more than a baby or a friend of his own age—here is a divine Friend who fills him with wonder and at the same time stirs his affection. But all the same, a child-God satisfies only part of his psychological and spiritual needs. Such a figure expresses only one aspect of God and only very imperfectly conveys his majesty. It encourages the child's development less than the idea of God as an adult and with the standing of a grown man. A religion revolving around 'baby Jesus' does not orient the child towards that ideal which is embodied for him in the life of grown-ups. It keeps God and the child in the world of childhood and contributes to the building up of a partition between his world and that of adults, between his present and his future religion. Even if it is advisable to give some place in the child's religion to devotion to the Child Jesus, it should not—as far as we can control it (for God is free in his gifts)—be given an exaggerated importance, let alone the whole field.

Not the littleness, but the glory and majesty of Jesus should be presented to the child, and when it is not Christmas time, let us show Jesus in his older boyhood and manhood and his glorious life in Heaven. Jesus should really be the 'Lord Jesus' for the child.[1]

MYSTERIES OF JESUS DURING THE LITURGICAL YEAR   Nevertheless, this Lord is a true friend. The child will become conscious of this friendship if, in some of the mysteries of the Saviour which he comes to know in the course of the liturgical year, care is taken always to associate the majesty of Jesus with his great goodness to those around him.

At Christmas, Jesus comes to us from Heaven in order to help us. This can be presented as God himself coming to us or, even better, we can present 'the Lord Jesus' as the 'Son of God', 'the King', whose coming from Heaven was foretold (or

---

[1] The angel Gabriel called him 'Jesus', but at the same time said 'He shall be great' and 'his kingdom shall have no end', and St Elizabeth a few lines further on in the Gospel of St Luke, calls him 'My Lord' (Luke I, 43). It should be realized that the word 'Jesus' to those to whom it was announced, meant 'Jahweh saves'; so it contained within it the name given to the Lord, and hence evoked a sense of majesty which not even the name 'Jesus' conveys to our ears.

as the 'Saviour' long awaited and sent by God).[1] This second presentation is more in keeping with the actual text of the story in the Gospel and, without making too much distinction between Jesus and God (the expression 'Son of God' should not be explained) it has the advantage that it does not say all at once and without qualification that Jesus is God : the two expressions, 'Lord Jesus' and 'Son of God', associated with the marks of respect with which the Child Jesus is surrounded from his birth, will bring his divine glory sufficiently in evidence.

At Nazareth, the Lord Jesus becomes for the child a friend of his own age, having the occupations of a child. The perfection of each of his actions, the admiration of his parents and the angels watching them will reveal his divine glory and goodness to the child.

In his public life (presented in one or two well-chosen scenes) the divine omnipotence of the Lord should be stressed in those acts of goodwill which show at the same time his great goodness and his friendship for men. Some words of Jesus' which the child can understand can be added here, especially on the love of God and the love of others.

On the Cross,[2] Jesus suffered bravely and died for us, be-

---

[1] The texts of Scripture authorize both these presentations, some speaking of God who will come to save his people, and others alluding to 'Him who will be sent' to carry out this work of salvation. It is possible to use the term Saviour even from this early age, as it is traditional in the Scriptures, but it is psychologically inadvisable to connect it with ideas of 'sin' and 'hell'. The word should be associated with the idea of a great Friend who comes to help mankind. The child has not yet acquired a sense of personal responsibility and is not capable of grasping what it means to sin; but on the other hand, he is constantly aware of his weakness and can well understand the need to have someone by him to help him to act well and to make him into a 'friend of God's'. Nevertheless some prefer to wait until the age of five or six before using the word 'Saviour'.

[2] Some may be surprised that we speak of the Cross to such young children. We are working here on the hypothesis that children living in a Christian environment will have already seen a Crucifix. Moreover, the Cross seems to have a mysterious attraction for many children once they know that it is Jesus on it. However this may be, whether one likes it or not, children will come into contact with the Cross. The important thing is that such contacts be constructive; we would like to add that in our experience the Cross, when presented with certain precautions, far from frightening the child and giving him a negative and depressing idea of religion, can be a wonderful

cause he loved us very much, but three days later he came
alive again to live forever, giving us the joy of Easter. We should
not insist on realistic details of his suffering. What the child
should know is that Jesus died out of love for him,[1] that he
was great and admirable (in courage, obedience, goodness, etc.)
in his death, and that he did not stay dead long, since he rose
again three days later to bring him and the whole world a
marvellous joy.[2]

From the time before Easter, therefore, the Resurrection will
have been always in the background and associated with the
Cross. After three days Jesus came alive again for always, his
glory is revealed, his return fills his friends with joy.[3]

From the Ascension, the Lord Jesus lives in glory in Heaven
with his Father, and he helps us from there, starting from

proof of the goodness and love of Jesus, a manifestation of his majesty, and a
source of joy.

Many children think of Jesus as dead because they have seen the Crucifix,
or because his death has been insisted on too much without a corresponding
insistence on his Resurrection. Oliver is sick and his mother suggests that
they pray to Jesus to make him better. Oliver replies: 'Jesus died first'.
How could someone dead make him better? So it is wise to emphasize the
fact of the Resurrection.

[1] For a young child the mere fact of doing something which requires effort for
someone is a proof of love, especially something very difficult. We could tell
the child more explicitly that Jesus died 'to show us that he loved us very
much'.

[2] This is the joy (Jesus' and ours) of the Resurrection, of being God's friends
and his children. There is a more detailed presentation of the Cross in the
programme (pp. 152, 154), based on the idea that Jesus died so that we could
all become better persons, fit to be friends of God. With this as a starting
point it is possible to connect the Cross to the two joys of Easter: the possibility
of divine friendship on earth and the hope of Heaven. Such a presentation
of the Cross contains the seed of all the elements of the mystery of the
Redemption. At this age, which is the age neither of reflection (around five)
nor awareness of sin (five to seven) it seems difficult and hardly advisable
to say more. The expression 'to save us', if one wants to use it does not mean
that we must necessarily speak of 'sin' or 'hell' (see note 1 above).

The explanation 'to open Heaven for us' will be very incomplete if it means
only a future Heaven; a point of view which postpones the benefits of the
Cross to the next life gives a false idea of Christian life; it is someone in the
present that the child needs, and he is quite capable, if helped by the faith of
those around him, of living in friendship with God already.

[3] Spiritual joy should reach its peak at Easter, both at home and at school.
This is not always the case. Practical suggestions are given in the programme
for the year, see below pp. 155-6, 158-9.

Pentecost, to become the Lord's friends on earth before taking us to Heaven to himself.[1]

So that we do not forget Jesus—all that he did for us on earth and his present friendship in Heaven—we put his picture on the wall. But Jesus has left us something much better than a picture to remember him by : his presence in the Tabernacle. With these children, who are not yet ready for Mass, nor for Communion, the presence of Jesus in the Tabernacle is an attractive sign of Jesus' friendship for him, so near and so mysterious at the same time.[2]

It can be hoped that by the end of a year lived with Jesus like this, within the framework of liturgical mysteries, a friendship will be formed between Jesus and the child in which adoration and familiarity will be harmoniously joined.

THE BLESSED VIRGIN

THE MOTHER OF THE LORD JESUS

The Blessed Virgin should be presented as the Mother of Jesus, not yet as the child's mother. Before Christmas, Mary's glory will become evident to the child as we tell him how the Angel Gabriel, sent by God, came to greet her and announce

---

[1] It may seem a little premature to speak of the Holy Spirit to children who have not yet reached the age of reflection and have hardly any idea of their own spirit. Isn't this to burden the child's mind unnecessarily and repress his religious life, rather than encourage it? Would it not be preferable, with children of three and four, to be satisfied with mentioning the presence of God or the help we receive from Jesus, but to wait for the age of reflection before mentioning the mysterious presence of the Holy Spirit within us, taking into account of course any special graces and the precocious development of certain children (here it is rather a question of individual education)? There does exist a way, however, of mentioning the Holy Spirit if one wants to, even at this age, and that is the one most often employed by God in the Bible: pointing to his presence through its sensible effects, for example through the effects of Pentecost on the Apostles (see pp. 166-7).

[2] On the way to present Jesus in the Blessed Sacrament at this age, see pp. 168-171. On the advisability of teaching this subject, see note 1, p. 168.

to her that she would be the mother of Jesus.[1] The presence
of the Blessed Virgin by the Crib, the pictures of her holding
the Child Jesus in her arms, will demonstrate her maternal
goodness as well as her greatness. By the end of the year the
child should know that she is in Heaven now, with the resurrected Jesus, and the angels and saints.

The child's prayer should consist of greeting Mary, expressing his joy like the angel, praising her, decorating her picture
(for a child to give flowers at this age is symbolically to give
himself), behaving well before God, like her, asking her help
to become, like her, a friend of our Lord Jesus.

THE ANGELS

Wonderful Beings Surrounding God, Praising and Serving Him

The angels should play a part in the picture that the child
of this age makes of divine things. Their presence contributes
to making God's extraordinary character known to him. Their
brilliant faces, white clothing, their songs in Heaven, their sudden appearance, their comforting presence near the child, are
so many wonderful images which delight him, help him
develop and give his religion an aura of heavenly light.

Their behaviour and prayer will be an example for him.
Their praise and adoration of God, their complete obedience in
his service, their admiration for the Lord Jesus and Mary will
help him in his adoration and love of God and his respect towards Jesus and the Blessed Virgin.

THE SAINTS

Great Friends of God and Jesus

The saints are God's great friends who on earth tried to do
everything like Jesus and who are now with him in Heaven.

---

[1] See the story of the Annunciation, p. 139-41.

Certain aspects of their life and some of their attitudes could help the child in his spiritual life : there he will find living examples of respect and love of God, friendship with Jesus, courage, and a burning desire to serve others; he will discover the love which God or Jesus shows his friends and acquire an idea of the friendship which God has for him.[1]

There should not be too many models, nor should the child's religion be founded on sand, that is to say on the lives of legendary saints. On the contrary, let us pick out those facts duly authenticated by the Church. Let us for preference look for inspiration in the Book of Saints, that is to say, the Bible, which is the source of Revelation, the religious book *par excellence,* which comes from God himself.

THE PEOPLE OF THE BIBLE

THE FRIENDS OF GOD TO WHOM THE LORD REVEALED HIMSELF

God revealed himself in a special way to certain men in times past, before revealing himself in the person of his Son, Jesus. This revelation was meant not only for those to whom it was directly given, but to all those who were called to be members of his people and his Church. It has been most faithfully preserved, under God's guidance, in the two parts of Scripture, the Old and the New Testaments, and it has been entrusted to the Church, for her to interpret for the good of her children. Our duty as teachers of religion is to point out to the child— under the Church's guidance—those things in divine revelation which are within everyone's scope and to seek out what can be useful and nourishing for his spiritual life.[2]

Now, what God has revealed in the course of his interventions into history in the Old Testament is essentially the mystery

[1] See for example the story of the transformation of the Apostles after the Ascension (pp. 166-7) and the conversion of St Paul (pp. 167-8).
[2] See Appendix I, pp. 172-4 below.

of his majesty inclining towards man, dealing with him with love in order to make him his friend; and in the New Testament it is his personal presence with us (here on earth and in Heaven) full of love and majesty, which makes us into his children. The child of three and four, equally sensible of the majesty, love and mystery, and needing the presence of someone near him, is actually capable of grasping what is essential in this revelation. Even more, his natural ability to identify himself with persons he sees or hears about in stories allows him to do the same with the persons in a religious story, better than we can do ourselves. The demonstrative religion of biblical figures makes them models particularly suited to the young child for whom physical action is necessary in order to grasp ideas. What is important is that those figures be chosen as examples who answered God's call with acts of religion imitable by a child of this age. In imitating their attitude and actions in a religious atmosphere, the child, helped by our faith, will acquire a genuinely religious spirit.

Figures from the Old Testament, like Moses, Abraham, Samuel, David, Solomon, Elias, in some episodes of their lives, can thus serve as models, as also can the Apostles, the Holy Women, the sick, the children mentioned in the Gospels. However, too many figures and episodes should not be presented to the child. It is of greater value to keep to a few persons who will become familiar as friends to him, to a few essential scenes, to a few fundamental attitudes.[1]

CREATION

God's Beautiful Gifts To the Child

God does not reveal himself to us only through the Scriptures but also through his creation—a way which a child can understand particularly well. The child of three and four is

[1] We give some indication in the programme of which scenes from the Scriptures can most profitably be presented to the child (p. 137).

not far from his beginnings and is still in harmony with everything that has to do with life. The spectacle of creation, of
living things especially, captivates him. In touch with nature,
his whole vitality is stimulated.

Here we have a natural method always at our disposal to
help the child to keep in contact with his God. In taking this
path, he will find God at work in the universe around him, at
the heart of his daily life. Without this intuition of God through
Creation, the child's religion will be greatly impoverished and
will lack realism : it will become a group of interests and pre-
occupations apart from his life, strange to the events of his
daily life, and outside the field of his needs and natural
interests.

The child lives in a world where there is the risk that the
incessant discoveries of science and technology will absorb all
the interest and energies of man. If we do not want his later
life completely cut off from God and deprived of religious
character, we should have him acquire from his earliest youth
the habit of seeing the work of God in all the riches of nature
and in all human values.

It is obviously not a question here of telling the child the
origin of the world according to Genesis, but of taking nature
itself as a starting point. Creation should mean for him all the
beautiful things in nature with which God has lovingly surrounded him.

We should take advantage of the opportunities which present
themselves to express admiration for light, flowers, water,
animals and give him the chance to watch, feel and enjoy at
his leisure, helping him even in this exploration and letting him
express his feelings freely, which will give him a feeling of unity
with us. It is when he is filled with these wonders that we should
raise his mind to God with a word of praise and thanks.[1]

The miracle of his own body is also part of nature to
be explored, and so are other human beings too—parents,
babies, etc. In this way the child can acquire the habit of

[1] See in the programme: 'The Joy of Spring' (p. 160).

perceiving the grandeur, beauty and goodness of God in everything that causes his admiration and wonder on earth and of
thanking God for it.

But God's absolute superiority over the whole of creation
should also be stressed at times: God is greater than everything, more beautiful than the flowers, stronger than the powerful waves of the sea, more wise than all the teachers in
the world.

PRAYER

The Child's Response in the Presence of God's Majesty and Goodness

Each revelation made to the child, each story, each of his
religious discoveries should end with a prayerful gesture, a
word, a turning towards God. This gesture, word, oft repeated
attitude, will gradually make God present in his life.

The child's prayer should be specially nurtured so that it
may become the means to a living contact with God. Let us
create an atmosphere which will allow the child to find God
in prayer. Let us choose the time and the place with care, and
let us learn to plan its form according to the changing liturgical
feasts. The child can be brought to silence by means of darkness or a light, or the tune of a hymn or a song or a small procession—or in many other ways. We should make him adopt
a respectful posture. The words we suggest to him for his
prayer should draw their inspiration from the Bible and the
Liturgy.

The example of Biblical figures or of certain gestures from
the Liturgy can be very helpful to the child in his prayer: he
will love to repeat Moses' greeting before God, covering his
eyes, or his prayer on the mountain with arms upraised, or the
angel's greeting to the Blessed Virgin, the Magi's prostration
before the Child Jesus, or to wave his arms, saying 'Alleluia'
or 'Hosannah', like the crowd on Palm Sunday.

Such ritual and somewhat solemn prayer is necessary, but the child should add his own personal and spontaneous prayer to it. He should acquire the habit of speaking to God of his own accord in the course of the day. At the beginning, his mother's or teacher's example may be necessary: 'I am going to say something to Jesus out aloud. Then you can say something too.' This could be thanks for the day just finished, praise to God for his creation, to Jesus for some incident of his life on earth, to the Blessed Virgin for her goodness, a prayer for some unfortunate person, a request for help or protection for oneself or for others. If the child refuses to pray aloud, one can say, for example, 'Let each of us tell Jesus on our own what we have done for him today'. And let us acquire the habit of expressing some words of prayer spontaneously before the child in the course of the day, without feeling obliged to wait for the time usually fixed for prayers in order to raise his thoughts to God.

MORNING PRAYERS   For a child of this age morning prayers might consist of taking a religious posture—hands joined, standing or kneeling—before some picture of a biblical scene or of Jesus, and making a deep bow, slowly, before God, perhaps adding some vocal prayer: giving his heart to the Lord, asking him to watch over him and all his family, praising God for his majesty and goodness in creation, for the feast of the day, for some event, repeating, for example, prayers learnt in class, or greeting the Blessed Virgin, like the angel Gabriel, with the first words of the 'Hail Mary'.

The prayers to God can be addressed as the case may be, to 'God', 'my God', 'Lord', or to 'Jesus', 'Lord Jesus', and very rarely except at Christmas time, to 'Baby Jesus'. Prayer should always end with a well-made salutation or, when the child has learnt it, with the sign of the Cross, made slowly and in silence.

NIGHT PRAYERS   With the same framework of ritual (silence, good posture, salutation) prayer at night can include thanks to God for the day, a request for a blessing for himself and the family (gradually widening to include all children and all men in the world), asking for protection for the night and for graces according to circumstances for himself or for others (with the child playing a personal part) or some other prayer as in the morning, related to the liturgical season. It can end with the angel's greeting to the Blessed Virgin and some aspirations to the saints and the angels.[1]

GESTURES   It is normal for gestures to accompany the prayer of a child of this age; but they will need a prepared atmosphere if they are to be taken seriously. This is more easily done in a class at school than at home, but it would be a pity if children used to praying with gestures in class should never do so at home. Parents should strive to achieve some continuity between prayer at home and at school.

Here are some examples as suggestions for gestures suitable to children of this age :

[1] Here, for example, is the kind of prayer suggested by Mlle Dingeon, of the institute for Formation Chretienne des Tout Petits in Paris for very young children (under the age of three) :
> "Good-night, God, Good-night Jesus,
> Good-night, Mother of Jesus,
> Good-night, angels and all the saints in Heaven.'

For children from three to six years of age, Mlle Dingeon makes the following suggestions :

'His prayer is not yet fully independent, but it can nevertheless begin to express other things than just greeting God, morning and evening. It can express happiness or sadness according to the circumstances; praise, requests, thanksgiving, offering. Not only "Good-night God" will be said but often "Thank you, my God", and "My God, I adore you", and in speaking this word which was unknown up to now, the child should bow down: this act will give the word meaning.

'He will say, "Please God, help me (to do such and such)"; or "make such a person well again". When anything is to be asked the prayer of petition should be preceded by "Please", "If you wish it for us".

'To improvised prayers, the traditional prayers of all Christians should be added from now on—the Hail Mary, Our Father, aspirations to the Patron Saints of the family, the Glory be to the Father, etc. (invocation to the Blessed Trinity)' (*Documentation Catechistique*, July 1955, pp. 28-29).

In our opinion, if a child prays alone, it is better to omit the Our Father and the last part of the Hail Mary until the age of five or six. But it is different in the case of younger children who pray with older ones. In this case, we should take care that each find something in the common prayers which is suitable to his age.

Head bent, while the children
—are standing up, sitting upright, or kneeling;
—have their hands joined together, or their head in their hands.

A low bow, while the children are
—standing up, their arms held close by the body,
—standing up, their hands joined,
—standing up, their arms slightly raised (the Angel's bow),
—standing up, or sitting down, their hands over their eyes (Moses' bow).

Complete prostration (not to be used very often)
—begun from the standing, kneeling, or sitting position,
—bowing slowly, hands joined,
—finishing with the forehead on the ground between the hands (the prostration of Solomon or of the Magi).

Gesture of announcing oneself at God's service
—the arms slightly raised, palms forward, head held up : 'Here am I Lord !' (The prayer of Abraham and Samuel).

Supplication
—arms raised towards heaven, like a child holding up his arms to his mother : ('Lord ! Lord !' the prayer of Moses on the mountain).

In thanksgiving or great joy
—arms flung up towards heaven in one movement : 'Thank you, Lord ! Hosannah ! Glory be to God ! Allelulia !'

In offering
—hold the hands in the gesture of offering used by the priest at Mass, then raise them slowly towards heaven.

Various feelings
—spread the arms out wide (idea of *grandeur*),
—make a circular movement with both arms (the idea of
    the *universe*),
—hands on heart (the idea of *goodness* and of *love*).

Words to use
(1) *to God:* (further prayers will be found in the programme
    for the year).

'God is great !' (arms spread wide).
'God is good !' (hands on heart).

The children can be led into the habit of always beginning
their prayer with some twofold acclamation of this kind for
example: *'O Lord, you are great! O Lord, you are good!'*

'My God, you are my King !' (Ps. 43 : 5).

'Heaven and earth are yours ! (circular gesture)
Day is yours
And night belongs to you' (Ps. 73 : 16).

'Lord, you are great.
Lord you are wonderful.
Lord you are strong.
Lord, you are the King of the whole world' (circular gesture).

'Lord, I will sing to you from my heart,
I will tell the story of all your marvellous deeds' (Ps. 9 : 2).

'Allelulia ! Praise the Lord !
Yes, God is powerful and everlasting,
Nothing is greater than God
And his kingdom will last for ever.
He is king from ocean to ocean
And to the very ends of the earth.
He is king of the whole universe.'

'With you, O Lord, I am not afraid.
I am as safe as a bird in its nest, as a lamb with its shepherd.'

'My God, when I am close to you
I am full of joy.
I keep very still,
I close my eyes,
I keep very quiet
And think of you.'
'Thank you, Lord, for the sun which shines, the lovely flowers,'
etc.

'O God, I am happy :
For your sake I was obedient' (or whatever other good deed
the child may just have done).

(2) *to Jesus:* (further prayers are to be found in the programme).

At Christmas tide :

'Lord Jesus has come to us !
Let us say with the angels :
Glory be to God in the highest ! (Arms raised to heaven)
Peace on earth to all men !' (Arms stretched wide).

At Eastertide :

'Jesus was dead,
But, see, he is alive ! Allelulia !'

After Pentecost :

'May the Lord Jesus be with us always !
Here am I, Lord Jesus, to be your friend !'

(3) *to our Lady:*

'Hail Mary (bowing low, like the Angel),
Full of grace (gesture of wonder),
The Lord is with you (hands together),
Blessed are you among women !' (stretching the arms wide).

'Holy Mary, mother of God (hands together),
Pray for us,
Pray for . . .' (naming various intentions).

THE SENSE OF GOOD AND EVIL

There is no need to wait for the age of moral responsibility in order to start orienting the child towards good. From the earliest age, the child should be told what is good and be encouraged to love it and to acquire the habit of doing good.

There should be no hesitation in a Christian environment in associating what is good with God. God loves and approves everything that is good. When we sense that a child is disposed to do some good action, let us say, 'God is watching you', but in a tone implying love and not surveillance, and after some activity, 'God loves you, and is pleased'. This watchfulness of God's over his actions, the joy of having pleased his Lord will be a spur to him. He will try to do well so that God will continue to look on him with love. Another positive and effective way of contributing to his education towards good is to point to the example of Jesus, a saint, or some biblical figure.

From his earliest years he should be taught to eschew evil. But evil should be mentioned in connection with God only with the greatest precaution. If he is told that God loves whatever is good, the child will understand of his own accord that what is bad will displease him, like being naughty, hitting others, disobeying. At this age we should still avoid mentioning 'sin' and talking about commandments and prohibitions given by God; he should not acquire the feeling of being guilty before God.

Although some conscious and voluntary malice can already insinuate itself into some of his acts, the child is not yet mature enough for us to be able to speak of real responsibility. More than anything else, he is at the mercy of his nature which needs to assert itself, and he does not yet possess enough mental detachment to reflect on his actions and stop them in time. His absolute need for love, moreover, makes it mandatory for us to avoid anything which might make him believe that he is not loved, and that God is angry with him.

So let us not say, 'God does not love you any more', and phrases such as, 'You have hurt Jesus very much', should be used only with a great deal of discretion. As he is not yet capable of distinguishing in his own conduct between what he is responsible for and what he is not responsible for, if the child is unable to avoid what is forbidden, or unable to do what God commands, he will inevitably feel that God looks on him with disapproval and that he is no longer loved.

If it be thought useful in the case of particularly religious children to mention occasionally God's disapproval of some bad action, it should be done in a general way: 'God does not like it, when children hit their little brothers.' It should be a judgment of the bad deed, not of the child who committed it and it should be made only in moments when the child is calm and in a receptive mood, that is to say, rarely at the time when the deed itself was done. The name of God should not enter into our rebukes. When a child does something wrong, he should certainly be stopped, and sometimes punished immediately, saying 'This is not allowed'; but there is no need to invoke the idea of God.

EFFORT

What we have said concerning education towards the good can by analogy be applied to education towards effort. We should not wait until the child is big to encourage him to make efforts, and to do this we can rely on his yearning to grow, his liking for the customary, his desire to imitate grown-ups. May he be thus encouraged to make efforts joyfully!

It is good to associate the thought of God with the child's efforts: he will be encouraged by God's approval and this will make the effort more attractive. At this age, however, there should be no demand for effort in connection with a religious idea. God should not be made to appear to a small child as an obstacle to his joy and development; otherwise with an instinctively defensive reaction a part of the child's nature will

turn away from God for life. If he is not up to making
the efforts which he thinks God demands of him, the child will
be tempted to break away from him. God's association with his
life should, on the contrary, exalt him.

The example of good and difficult actions done by others and
presented to him as worthy of a friend of God's may awaken
a desire in the child to imitate them. We have already mentioned how the example of our Lord and certain of the saints
can influence the child and even lead him to make certain
sacrifices, but remember the discretion with which this subject
must be treated.[1]

CHARITY

Can there be any question of educating a child to charity
at this age of self-assertion? Psychologists tend to see all the
child's actions, even those regarding others, as a way for him
to put himself forward or to show off: a favour done
to a grown-up is a way for the child to associate himself with
the adult on an equal footing, help to a younger child is a way
of showing his superiority.

Even granting this hypothesis, it is still educationally good to
orient the child's behaviour so that he will get into the habit
of considering others, of being helpful to those around him and
co-operating with them. Here again, his desire to grow and to
imitate grown-ups can be appealed to and to this natural reason
we can add the thought of God's loving and watchful approval
of those who are kind, and his pleasure in seeing the child use
the gifts he has given him (his hands, his body, etc.) in a good
way: this contact with God's majesty and the feeling that he
resembles Jesus will be most helpful to him.

But we have seen that his desire to grow is not the only
motive behind the child's acts: just as strong is his need for
love. In pleasing someone, the child does not seek only esteem
but also love. It is true that to rely solely on the child's emotional

[1] See pp. 71-2.

needs in order to get him to do good deeds is a wrong approach, which would encourage him to persist in the attitude and feelings of early infancy and put excessive emphasis on the influence of his emotions, which he should be learning by degrees to control. But after the event we can point out to him the love which his helpfulness merits; or, better, the joy it brings; and the child will be able to perceive this love in the joy of those around him, and the love and joy of God too: 'God saw that you were good to your little sister. He is pleased because he loves you.' By associating God's joy with that of his little sister, the child will gradually acquire the habit of seeing in his love of others a way of demonstrating his love to God.

It is true that at the age of three and four, the need for love is above all a need to be loved. It has been said above that a child who, at the age of two, easily shares everything he gets with his family because he does not yet distinguish between himself and them, will on the contrary experience great difficulties in considering others before his own personal wishes, once he has become conscious of his own individuality and acquired a sense of property. But it was seen, too, how in discovering his own personal will, he became conscious of the will of others. This discovery of other people's existence makes the beginnings of voluntary charity—a certain conscious and meritorious giving—possible, and at least allows for its education.

It would certainly be clumsy to ask too much of the child, whose first need is to assert himself in order to grow and become 'someone'. Nevertheless it is possible to draw him discreetly into this difficult path by our example, associating him with our own charitable acts and sentiments, and his religion should also make him feel some obligation to consider others. In the course of stories from the Scriptures or while observing nature, we can tell the child that God loves each of his children and by pointing out God's loving watchfulness over others as well as over him, we can implant images and feelings of goodwill in his mind which will allow God's grace to bring the seeds of true charity to fruition.

But nothing will equal the example of our Lord Jesus in this respect : his goodness in the Crib, for rich and poor, big and small, his compassion for the humble, the sick, the unfortunate in his public life, his loving kindness towards children, and above all, the sight of his Cross, his suffering and his death undertaken willingly for love of us : all this can stimulate the child to feelings, words and acts of charity which are beyond nature.

As in other fields of his education, the example of Jesus will make sense and come alive for the child only through the mediation of parents and teachers who, through their own example, imbued with faith, are able to make known to him what Christian charity can be, that is to say charity joyful and patient, at the service of all, drawing its strength from prayer and meditation in the presence of God and of Jesus, our Lord.

PART THREE

A YEAR'S PROGRAMME FOR
RELIGIOUS EDUCATION
IN THE CLASS OR AT HOME

OUTLINE

THIS PROGRAMME is given simply as an example of how to apply in practice what we have said in the first two parts of this book. There are many possible programmes which can be devised; all presuppose for their success that the principles outlined above have been understood and are put into practice. This programme is best suited to children of four or five years old; for three-year-olds it needs adaptation and simplification. It was originally devised for classroom use in an infant school, but can be adapted for use at home.

As we have seen in our study of the psychology of the little child, he has a need to explore the outside world, which seems wonderful to him, he needs to raise himself to the level of the grown-ups around him, and in order to grow and flourish, he needs affection. The religious programme which we outline in the following pages tries to answer these needs by bringing the child into contact with the greatness of God and his extraordinary love and mercy, through stories taken from the Old and New Testaments : these stories must be told by the adult in an atmosphere of religious awe, and should gradually transform the life of the child, whether he is at school or at home, and help him to be 'one of God's friends', following in the steps of the characters from the Bible whom he comes to know.

While we lay stress here on stories from the Bible, the necessity of revealing God from creation and from the everyday life of the child should never by forgotten.[1] What we must seek is that balance between the revelation of God through the Bible and the discovery of God in daily life which will make the child's religion realistic.

At the outset (Chapter 1), we shall try to introduce the child to God through stories taken from the Old Testament, so that from the very beginning of his religious education he will be filled with respect for divine power and greatness. This grandeur should from the very beginning be permeated with goodwill so as to touch the young Christian and inspire him to love and adore God and to want to become his friend. This will provide us with the opportunity of showing the presence of God in his life, as well.

Christmas, with our Lord's birth, will show the child this great God giving himself with great love to men.

At a later stage (Chapter 2), the Lord Jesus will be presented to him, so that his goodness and majesty will captivate him as well as draw him on to develop in contact with him. Near Jesus, the child will learn to please God.

The suffering on the Cross, with the stress on the Lord's goodness and courage, will of itself affect the child and help him to become more generous.

At a third stage (Chapter 3), our Lord, resurrected, returning among his friends, will give the child the joy of both his triumph and his return, which nature itself seems to share with the coming of spring. The ascension of Jesus into heaven, the help he continues to give his friends on earth, the discovery of his presence in the Tabernacle will contribute to maintaining his joy and generosity and he will go on discovering the joys of creation at the same time.

A friendship can form between the child and our Lord, encouraged by the example of the saints, which will add spiritual gladness to his life and transform into an active love of God and others his desire to grow up.

[1] See below, p. 160 ff., and Appendix II.

1 THE FIRST STAGE— LEADING UP TO CHRISTMAS

WE BRING THE CHILD INTO CONTACT WITH THE MYSTERY OF GOD'S MAJESTY AND GOODNESS

PREPARATION

THIS PREPARATION will consist of teaching the child gradually to control himself and to be silent and in the creation of an atmosphere which is full of respect, friendliness and joyfulness. This has already been discussed above in Part I (pp. 25-7). It should be stressed, however, that in order to achieve real silence and a certain degree of attention and concentration on the child's part, it is not enough to practise silence now and then, going directly from a state of excited activity to calmness: on the contrary, the normal atmosphere should be such, that silence comes naturally. This atmosphere can be achieved by countless small acts, done calmly and with dignity, which will inculcate the habit of self-control, regularity, and order in the child's life and will be some preparation for silence. He should be asked to keep his clothes tidily (hang them up or fold them when he takes them off or changes), put each thing in its place, speak politely to others, especially to older people, not disturb other people's work. The habit of consciously doing certain acts well is an excellent preparation for the spiritual life for a small child.

But this education in self-control and silence must not convey the feeling of constraint or be carried out in an atmosphere of gloom : this would indeed be a sorry introduction to a religion of love, and in total contradiction to the living God, source of all life and all joy, whom we wish the child to come to know. On the contrary, let us be joyful, friendly and good-humoured : each child should feel our understanding and the warmth of our friendship for him, our goodwill, even when we are being firm; and our respect should never convey coldness of feeling.

When a child seems capable of silence and respect, we can tell him that now the time has come when he can begin to learn about God. He should have the feeling that now he is big enough and good enough to be allowed to know something of a delightful secret.

The stories which follow (they are intended as suggestions) should be prayerfully meditated on before they are told, so that something of our faith may be conveyed to the child. They should be told in an atmosphere of respectful silence and be made as vivid and dramatic as possible for the small child by telling them with expression and acting them out for him (by becoming Moses ourselves, covering our face with our hands, bowing down). This helps the child identify himself with the central figure and assimilate the lesson that the story is giving. Each story is followed by a short commentary, explaining what we want the story to convey, and helping the child to make it part of his life and translate it into practical action. A short prayer is added at the end, in keeping with the spirit of the story.

It is suggested that each story be repeated on different occasions until the child has understood it, before going on to the next one, and in the case of longer stories, that they be broken up into two parts, as suggested in the text, if they seem too much for one occasion.

1. Moses' Vision of the Burning Bush (Exodus 3 : 1-9)

God's majesty is revealed to Moses in his solitude.

One day, children, a man heard God speaking to him. This man was called Moses.

Moses was a shepherd and he was alone on a mountain with his sheep. He was sitting on the ground in silence.

Moses was feeling very sad. He thought : 'God has left me. I am all alone. I have no one to help me.'

Suddenly, raising his head, Moses saw a great flame in the middle of a bush and he got up to see what this great flame was.

But while he was walking towards it, he heard Someone calling him from the middle of the flame, 'Moses! Moses!' (*Silence*). It was God calling him :

Moses answered, 'Here I am!'

'Do not come near here!' God said to him, 'Take off your shoes. It is I, God, your God, who am here. I have come to you to help you'.

'God! My God!' Moses said to himself.

Then Moses took off his shoes, hid his face in his coat and bowed down low before God.

You have seen how low Moses bowed down before God, when he knew that it was God—his God—who was calling him from the great flame. We are going to stand up straight too and be very silent. Then we shall put our hands in front of our eyes and we shall bow down before God like Moses did, with our eyes closed and keeping very still.

EXPLANATION   In the first telling of this story there is no need to go into details about the unhappy state of God's people in Egypt; we should concentrate the child's attention entirely on the two characters : God and Moses. We have translated the expression 'I am the God of Abraham, of Isaac and of Jacob' (i.e., of your family) by 'your God', since at this age the child is effectively one with his family. For the same reason, we have symbolized the sadness of the Chosen People by Moses' sadness, and God's promise of help to his people by his promise to Moses.

FOLLOW-UP   1. Repetition : Every day for the next fortnight
                or so, tell this story again : either the whole
story or some detail from it; make again, with the children,
Moses' 'low bow', in the same atmosphere of reverence. By
the retelling of the story, and by this repeated bow, the child
will become physically aware of the grandeur of God.

2. Wall picture : The display of a really good illustration,
coloured, restrained, truly religious in feeling and imaginative,
either at home or in the class room, can be very useful in re-
calling to the child Moses' reverence before God, and can help
in the formation of his faith.

3. Activity : After a few days, when the child has had time
to absorb the story and this picture, he can make his own drawing of the incident, take it home (if he is at school), or show it
to the whole family (if he has heard the story at home).

4. Comment : After the story has been told several times,
one can point out, with restraint, some aspect or other of Moses'
behaviour : for example, his silence, his sadness, his reply to
God, his great joy, his deep bow . . .; or, perhaps, comment on
the image of the flame, or on the words God used; all this is
done so that the child thinks actively about the incident, it lives
in his mind, and by imitating Moses' attitudes, they will gradually become a part of his own personality.

In connection with the words 'God ! My God !', point out
that the 'Lord of heaven and earth' (using a wide circular
gesture) was close to Moses. This is an expression with which
the child will need to be familiar before he comes to the second
story.

In class or at home, practise being very silent, and holding
oneself very still, at prayer time.

Throughout all of this, the dominant impressions should be
of God's greatness. But do not neglect to point out Moses'
joy at the thought that God had come to his aid.

Now is the time to point out the human reason for Moses'
sorrow : that his family, in a far country called Egypt, were
unhappy because they were badly treated by a wicked king.

Do not stress the king particularly, lest he should overshadow Moses and God himself.

Note: This is the method to follow in telling each of the stories that we will introduce the children to during the course of the year: repetition, illustration, dwelling on one point or another, (never spending more than 3-5 minutes at any one time on the subject) always in the same atmosphere of silence and respect. Never take more than one story per week, and the longer the child can profitably dwell with one story, the better.

2. GOD PROMISES TO HELP MOSES (Exodus 3: 10-12; 4: 10-13, 20)

Moses was silent before God.

God said to him: 'Moses, go to the king of Egypt, the Pharaoh, and tell him that he must let you leave the land of Egypt with all your family and all your friends.'

But Moses was afraid of the king of Egypt, the Pharaoh, who was a bad king. Moses said to God: 'Lord, I am afraid of the Pharaoh, send someone else to him.'

God said to him: 'Do not be afraid of the Pharaoh. I will be with you, I, the Lord. Go to Pharaoh.'

But Moses was afraid ... (repeat the last two paragraphs three times, ending the third time with: 'I, the Lord of Heaven and of earth.')

Then Moses set out to go to the Pharaoh, and on the way he said to himself:

'God the Lord of Heaven and earth, will be with me. With God I am not afraid!'

And he continued to walk, repeating the same words to himself, 'God ...' (repeat)

Moses was right. God is stronger than everyone, stronger than the Pharaoh and all the kings; with God there is no need to be afraid of anyone or of anything!

Prayer:

'God is the Lord of Heaven and earth!
He is stronger than all kings!
With God there is no need to be afraid!'

Come back to the Prayer several times commenting on it

during the week. Act out the way Moses walked fearlessly towards Egypt; the child will gradually come to see what it
means to be one of God's friends.

3. GOD SHOWS HIS POWER TO THE PHARAOH (Exodus 5 : 1-2; 6 : 1; 9 : 22, 27-28)

Moses set out and arrived at the Pharaoh's house. He went
in, greeted the Pharaoh, and said to him : 'God, the Lord,
has sent me to tell you that you must let me leave Egypt with
all my family and all my friends.'

The Pharaoh replied : 'I do not want to let you leave Egypt
with your family and all your friends. Go away !' And he made
Moses leave his house.

Then Moses raised his hands to God and said, 'Lord, see !
The Pharaoh will not obey you. He will not let us leave Egypt.'

God answered him : 'Do not be afraid for I am here. The
Pharaoh will see that I am the Lord, and he will obey me, you
will see !'

And God commanded the sky to send great clouds over the
Pharaoh's country and let a great hail storm rage over the
land so that Pharaoh would obey.

The Pharaoh, seeing the great clouds coming in the sky, and
the great hail storm over his country, said to himself : 'God is
great ! God is strong ! He is the Lord ! I must obey him !'

And the Pharaoh said to Moses : 'Yes, I will let you leave
Egypt with your family and all your friends.'

Now you will understand, children, that Moses was very
happy, and in his heart he said to God :

'Thank you, Lord !
You are great !
You are strong ! Stronger than all kings !
Stronger than all men !'

Or,

'Truly, you are the Lord of Heaven and earth !'

God is really great and strong, children. He can command
the sky and the earth, and they obey him. Everyone and everything must obey him. We shall pray like Moses :

'Lord, you are great ! . . . .'

This story should be commented on, emphasizing not only the majesty, but also the goodness and love of God which it illustrates. On different occasions different commentaries can be used :

> Yes, God is great and everything obeys him. He can command the clouds, the rain, thunder, the mountains, the sea. He is the master of everything, and everyone has to obey him, even kings.

Or,

> Yes, God is good. He did not leave his friend Moses all by himself, he came to him to help him. It was to help Moses that he sent the hail storm, and he made the Pharaoh afraid so that he would let Moses leave Egypt with his family and all his friends. God is always near his friends, and looks after those who love him. He listens to those who speak to him and helps those who ask him.

'OUR FATHER IN HEAVEN' Once the child seems to have assimilated the spirit of this story he can be helped to see God's action in the happy events of his life, and, without forcing him in any way, gradually come to call God his 'Father in Heaven'.

4. GOD COMES TO SPEAK TO MOSES IN A TENT (Exodus 12 : 31, 37; 25 : 8-9; 23 : 1, 7-17; 40 : 34-38)

1.—Pharaoh obeyed God. He let Moses leave Egypt with all his family and his friends and they went away from there.

But they did not know the way. They were afraid of the people who might attack them on the way and not let them pass. But God was there and was still watching over them.

Moses turned to God and said: 'Lord, come with us and help us !'

God answered : 'I will come with you and help you, but you must build a great tent for me, and I will always be with you to help you.'

Moses and his friends made a beautiful tent for God and they put it up in a place where it was very silent.

2.—Then Moses went all alone into God's tent, to speak to the Lord in the silence.

The moment that Moses came into the tent, a great cloud came down from the sky and stood still before the door of the tent. In the cloud there was light.

Moses' friends, seeing the great cloud with the light in it said : 'It is the Lord, who has come.' And they bowed themselves down to the ground before God, and did not move.

Yes, children, it was the Lord who came to speak to Moses. And in God's tent Moses spoke to the Lord.

It was a great joy for Moses to speak to God.

PRAYER When this story has been understood and accepted by the child, it can be pointed out to him how happy Moses was to be with God (the Lord of Heaven coming to him who is only a man !); his way of bearing himself, his silence, his reverential greeting, his way of speaking to God and listening to him : God spoke to him as a 'friend speaking to his friend' (Exodus 33 : 11). To the theme, 'God's friend', is added a new element : how a friend of God's prays.

Each day, Moses came to this house of silence to speak to God (perhaps here, to indicate a likeness to the child's own prayer, we could begin using the word 'Prayer')—From now on, the Lord stayed with them, and each time that Moses had something to tell him or something to ask, he could go to God's tent to speak with him.

Prayer:

'The Lord is good !
He loves us greatly
And watches over us !'

adding perhaps, if the child is prepared, 'He is our Father in Heaven !', and some other prayer drawn from the Psalms, which speaks of the presence of God amongst those who love him : e.g., 'The Lord hears those who pray to him,

And is near those who love him' (Ps. 144, 18, 19, adapted).

From its very beginning, the child's prayer should turn towards praise and thanks as well towards asking for help. This will be easy if one has already started to point out God's action in his life to him.

It can be explained why God asked for a house to be made especially for himself where it was silent, and a special place can be set aside (at home or at school) as an oratory, the place set aside for prayer.

With some children could be mentioned even at this stage the joys of Heaven, where we shall not only be with God, but see him in all his beauty and glory, like the angels. Here, we could tell them of the prayer of the angels in the vision of Isaiah, and say it together: 'Holy, holy, holy is the Lord!', bowing down. However, Heaven is treated in a later part of this programme.

5. SOLOMON, THE SON OF KING DAVID, BUILDS A GREAT AND BEAUTIFUL HOUSE FOR GOD (I Chron. 17: 1-2; 22: 2-19; II Chron. 2: 5; 3: 1; 6: 12-21, 40-41; 7: 1-3, 6)

1. A king who was called David loved God very much. One day he wanted to do something especially beautiful for the Lord: he wanted to make him a great and beautiful House— a real house made of stone, and not just one made of material like the tent.

King David asked everyone to bring beautiful stones and precious wood and gold to make God's House; then he called his son, Solomon, and said to him: 'Solomon, my son, you are going to build God's House.'

And Solomon built the House of God as his father King David asked him to do, and it was as high as a mountain.

2. When God's house was finished, Solomon looked at it and was very happy in himself, it was so beautiful and so big.

Then Solomon knelt down, raised his hands to God and said: 'Lord, see the House I have made for you. I am giving it to you. Come quickly to this House and stay with us for ever.'

At this moment, a great flame came down from the sky and

a great cloud filled God's House. It was the Lord who had
come into the House that Solomon had built for him.

Then Solomon said : 'The Lord is there ! The Lord is there !'
And he bowed down right to the ground.

And everyone bowed down to the ground too, saying :

'Let us sing to the Lord,
For he is good,
For he loves us forever.'

Solomon stood up again and everyone sang with him :

'Let us sing etc.'

Music was played and they all sang again.

'Let us sing to the Lord. . . .'

OFFERING   When talking this story over with
SOMETHING TO GOD the children, the joy of doing some-
                  thing for God can be pointed out—
God's joy at the *offering,* and the joy of God's friend in the
doing of it, which was what Solomon felt in building God's
House. The concept, 'God's friend' is now widened to include
the offering of things to God and the search for what is pleasing
to him.

An offering to make to God, at home or at school, at this
stage, should consist essentially of some material activity
(drawing or some other activity which the child usually does)
rather than some spiritual thing. If it has not already been
done, an altar could be set up in the corner set aside for prayer,
and the children could bring their offerings and set them on it.
Again, Heaven could be mentioned as the true House of God,
more beautiful than all churches, if it seems opportune.

A VISIT TO THE   The preceding scene gives a good oppor-
LORD'S HOUSE   tunity to prepare for a visit to a church or
                 chapel. It should only be done if the child
or children seem sufficiently prepared for it. There is no need
to speak of the presence of Jesus in the Tabernacle yet; the
best method of making children conscious of the presence of
God is an attitude of the greatest respect. A class of children

could sing an appropriate hymn before entering in silence. A great bow of reverence, made in silence, is however, enough to expect in the Church itself.

INTRODUCING   These can be presented as the prayers made to
THE PSALMS   God by King David, who sang them before the
              Lord. For instance, to tell God that he was not afraid when God was near him, he sang, 'The Lord is my Shepherd . . .' (Ps. 22).

From this time on, we could teach some verses from the Psalms, adapted and chosen to suit the ideas we want to convey. We have already mentioned Psalm 144, which is a pattern for prayer. Solomon's prayer in the Temple brings to mind Psalm 135.

6. OTHER STORIES FROM THE SCRIPTURES WHICH SHOULD
     BE USED TO INTRODUCE THE CHILD TO GOD IN HIS
     MAJESTY :

Moses on Sinai (Exodus 24 : 12-18; 19 : 10-11, 16-20).
Jacob's ladder (Genesis 28 : 10-15).
Agar in the desert (Genesis 21 : 14-20).
Abraham obeys God (Genesis 12 : 1-4).
Abraham builds an altar to thank God (Genesis 12 : 7-8;
     13 : 4, 18).
Samuel hears the voice of God (Samuel, 3 : 2-10).
Elias is visited by God (I Kings 19 : 11-13).

Note : It is not necessary to use all these stories. But if the child seems to lack the right attitude to prayer, one or more of these stories can be used, in the manner we have already indicated, as the rest of this programme proceeds, we must always draw out in the telling of these stories, the religious attitude which the child can in some way make his own.

GOD IN HIS GREATNESS
DRAWS NEAR TO THE CHILD

The following stories are intended as a preparation for Christmas, the feast of God's coming to us. With children of this age this preparation should not be started more than a fortnight ahead.

1. ANNOUNCING THE COMING OF CHRISTMAS

Soon, children, we shall have the feast of Christmas. This is the feast of the birth of our Lord, Jesus, of his coming on earth. It was on the night of Christmas that Jesus was born, a little baby in the Crib, and there was great joy in Heaven and on earth because of it. Every year, to remember this great joy when Jesus was born and came to us, we keep the feast of Christmas. It is a great joy for all God's friends on earth.

THE IDEA OF CHRISTMAS Use the phrase 'Feast of Christmas' several times, and add that 'it is a time of great joy for all God's friends'. It is worth going over these ideas frequently, and getting the children themselves to express them, in order to help them to have a true picture of what Christmas is. The most valuable way of instilling this idea is through the preparation of the Crib.

In working with children who have as yet very little idea of Jesus, the concept of Christmas could be introduced rather differently : Jesus could be presented as the most marvellous present that God could ever have given us. Speak of him as the 'Son of God', the 'friend of the whole world', 'come from heaven to live with us and help us'. Make this the time of joyful waiting for him who came to be our friend.

The Custom of preparing the Crib is often neglected even in religious families in English-speaking countries, all the attention being concentrated on the coming of Santa Claus, the Christmas Tree and dinner. Some effort should be made to re-introduce the custom and make our Lord's birth again the centre of our activities. There is no need to go to the extreme of abolishing the more secular aspects of Christmas all together: what is more fitting than presents on the feast of Christ's birth, through whom all gifts come to us? or more natural than a lighted Christmas tree, symbolic of the light (both natural and supernatural) that begins to increase at this time? (In our electrified age we are not so sensitive to natural phenomena as were people in times past, who saw a religious significance in the increase of the sun's light.) The evergreen tree itself is symbolic of the hope of Spring and Easter. All those things can have a religious significance: for instance the carol 'The Holly and the Ivy' where originally pagan symbols are given a Christian meaning.

Santa Claus or Father Christmas presents a more difficult problem perhaps for those who do not wish to abolish him. They would do well to consider whether the joy which a child gets from believing a legend literally is worth the risk of breaking down, or at least weakening, his trust in his parents. If, however, Santa Clause reverts to St Nicholas, giving gifts out of love of God, and if his coming on Christmas night is presented as a legend (. . . and some people say that he still goes around giving gifts . . .) without any insistence on this as a fact, it can probably be well integrated into religious celebration of Christmas and at the same time avoid (and this is probably what many parents fear most) making the child too 'different' from others around him.

2. GOD SENDS AN ANGEL TO THE BLESSED VIRGIN (Luke 1 : 26-29)

Soon we shall have the feast of Christmas, the feast of the time when Jesus was born on earth. Now I want to tell you how God sent an angel to Mary, the mother of Jesus, to tell her that Jesus was going to be born.

Mary was a young girl living in a village. God had made her very, very good, better than all other women in the world. She was filled with the Light of God and because she was so good we call her the Blessed Virgin.

One day God sent an angel from Heaven, the Angel Gabriel,

to the Blessed Virgin to tell her something very special. He told her that Jesus was going to be born and that God wanted her to be his mother. The Blessed Virgin did not know this yet.

The angel came into Mary's room. He saw her filled with God's Light and she was so beautiful that he greeted her saying : 'Hail Mary ! Full of grace, the Lord is with you. You are blessed amongst all women.' And he bowed down before her.

The words the angel said to Mary are very beautiful and we shall say them to her too, and bow down to her like he did.

A picture or a statue of the Blessed Virgin should be shown to the children, if this has not already been done and the Angel's greeting said before it. In the course of the week, we should come back to this scene and dwell on the Angel's words.

Something should be said about Mary's goodness, perhaps even touching on the fact that the Light of God within her is God himself, explaining something of the meaning of the phrases 'full of grace' and 'blessed amongst women'. What should be stressed is that she is the greatest of God's friends and was always so from the time she was born, because God wanted her to be the mother of Jesus.

3. The Angel Tells Mary That Jesus is to be Born (Luke 1 : 30-35)

This story should be told before the Crib is set up.

But the angel did not come only to greet Mary. God sent him to tell her some great news. What news?

At first, when she saw the angel coming into her room, Mary was afraid. But the angel said to her: 'Do not be afraid, Mary. I have come to tell you great news :

> You are to become the mother of a child.
> This child will be called Jesus,
> He will be the Son of God,
> And will be a great King forever.'

Then the angel left.

Mary stayed, in silence. She was very happy because Jesus was going to be born at Christmas : he was going to come to us to be our friend, and a friend to everyone, big and small, rich and poor.

And Mary said with great happiness (join the hands) :
> 'The Lord Jesus will come amongst us,
> He is the Son of God !
> He will be a great King forever ! (arms spread wide)
> He will be the Friend of all men !'

This last can be said as a prayer and repeated every day during the week. Turn the child's thoughts and his heart towards the feast of Christmas.

PREPARING   The child should be allowed to help in getting the
THE CRIB   Crib ready. With more than one child, each
          should be allowed to bring something (collect moss, get straw) and do something (put the stable together, arrange animals or shepherds, etc.), towards the whole thing, so that he can feel that he too is doing something and offering something to the Christ-Child, identifying himself more readily with the figures around the Manger.

4. THE BIRTH OF OUR LORD JESUS (Luke 2 : 1-7)

The time came when our Lord, Jesus, was to be born in Bethlehem.

It was the night of Christmas. The Blessed Virgin with Saint Joseph was waiting in silence near the Manger prepared for the coming of the Child Jesus. In heaven all the angels were waiting too, watching the Manger in Bethlehem.

Suddenly, thousands of angels sang :
> 'Glory to God in the Heavens !
> And peace on earth to all men !'

The child Jesus had been born on earth. His mother was holding him in her arms with great love.

Mary and Saint Joseph were filled with happiness as they looked at him.

With great care they laid him in the Manger. They stood before him in silence and with great respect, saying to themselves :
> 'Our Lord Jesus is born.
> He has come to us from Heaven.
> He is the Son of God !
> He will be our King forever,
> And the Friend of all men !'

It is good to tell this story standing before the Crib, with the candle lit, and to pray, using the words of the angels and Mary and Joseph. Perhaps some simple carol that the children know should be added. With this we begin to associate the presence of Jesus with light, especially through the use of candles around the Crib while we pray.

2 THE SECOND STAGE: FROM CHRISTMAS TO EASTER

THE AIM now is to bring the child to realize the greatness and goodness of the Lord Jesus: his greatness, so that the child may feel respect for him, and feel his own personality developing; his goodness, so that the child will want to give himself to the Lord.

The child, hearing from the stories we tell him how others have behaved when close to Jesus' greatness and goodness, will feel within himself the stirring of those religious feelings of wonder and love, awareness and trust, permeated with adoration, which one should feel in Jesus' presence. If these feelings are to strike deep roots, each incident from the life of Christ should be dwelt on and retold, in the way we have already detailed, for at least one week.

Also, during these months after Christmas, take the opportunity to point out the beauties of nature, teaching the child to appreciate the warmth and comfort of home in contrast to the cold outside, and so on, and to thank God for these things.

THE GREATNESS OF THE LORD JESUS AS A CHILD

1. THE SHEPHERDS COME TO KNOW JESUS (Luke 2: 8-20)

On the night of Christmas, some shepherds were resting in the fields, looking after their sheep. Suddenly a great light came from the sky and an angel appeared to them. The shepherds were greatly astonished. He told them that Jesus, our Saviour (or, our Friend), the great King, had come from Heaven to help us. And a great number of angels appeared, singing :

'Glory be to God in the highest !
And on earth peace to all good men !'

The shepherds rejoiced greatly and went to the Manger the angels had told them of and they knelt down and adored him in silence. Then they prayed :

'Our Lord Jesus is born.
He has come from Heaven to be with us.
He is the Son of God,
And our King forever,
And the Friend of all men !'

The children can act this out, imitating the shepherds at rest, the angels' song, the walk through the night, etc. They can repeat, at prayer time, the angel's song. During the day, help them to please Jesus.

2. THE THREE KINGS COME TO JESUS (Matt. 2 : 1-12)

The three Kings, friends of God, were waiting for the Great King who was to come from Heaven. They were watching the sky to see the star, which would announce his coming. When they saw the star, their joy was great and they set out to follow where it would lead them. And it led them to the place where Jesus was born. It stopped and shone over the Manger in Bethlehem. The Kings rejoiced and bowed down before the child, and kneeling they said :

'Here is Jesus, our Lord !
Here is the King of Heaven come down to us !
Glory to Jesus !
Glory to the King of Kings !'

And they gave him gifts of gold, frankincense and myrrh.

This too can all be acted out on several different occasions. Bring in the action of offering something precious to the Lord. Discuss what the child, at home or at school could offer : a job well done, a toy for poor children, good behaviour . . . his heart.

3. JESUS IS PRESENTED IN THE TEMPLE (Luke 2 : 22-23)

In Jerusalem there was a great servant of God, Simeon, who did not yet know that Jesus had been born. Each day he went into the house of God to see if the Saviour had come. He said to himself: 'When the Saviour and King whom we are all waiting for has come, there will be great joy for everyone, and a great light over all the earth.'

One day, Mary brought the child Jesus to God's house when Simeon was there; he saw the child and it gave him great happiness to see him at last. He took the Child from his mother, held him in his arms and said to God :

> 'Thank you, O God ! (*or* You are blessed, O God !)
> For I have seen Jesus with my own eyes,
> Jesus, who is the light of the world
> And the Saviour and Friend of all men.'

Then take the baby from the crib, hold it up as Simeon did the child, and get the child to repeat a prayer something like Simeon's : e.g.

> Blessed Be God.
> Jesus has come down from heaven
> to help all men.
> Jesus is a great light, and gives light
> to the whole world.

Next day, go over this story again. Explain how Lord Jesus lights up every man's heart and is the great light for the whole world. Let each child light a candle or lantern from the candles round the crib, saying several times the prayer above, or something more simple, such as 'Lord Jesus, you are my light and my joy.' All this will link the ideas of light and joy with the presence of Jesus. Light a candle at the place where prayers are usually said in his honour. Thank God (as Simeon did) for the joy of having seen Jesus. Pray that every child in the world may have this joy.

Go on to teach the child how everything he does can be like a light shining in honour of Jesus, a light which God prefers to any candle.

JESUS AT NAZARETH

Although it is fitting, at this age when the child admires and looks up to adults, to tell him about Jesus as a man, do not neglect to show him our Saviour as a child of his own age. Spend at least two weeks on the life of Jesus with Mary and Joseph—but do not invent all sorts of imaginary details to fill out the picture.

1. JESUS AT NAZARETH WITH MARY (Luke 2 : 39-40, 51-52)

Jesus grew up and became a big boy, walking and talking and running about.

At home in Nazareth, he stayed near his mother, the Blessed Virgin. Everything he did, he did properly. When his mother asked him to do something for her he said 'yes' straight away, and he tried to help everyone in any way he could (for example, getting the water they needed from the well which was far away and bringing it home in a pitcher).

Mary watched him, and seeing how well he did everything he had to do, and always said 'yes' when asked to do anything, and was always kind, she was very pleased and said to herself :

'Jesus is great and does all things well !
He is good and helps everyone !'

And the angels in Heaven prayed the same prayer.

It can be stressed when enlarging on this during the week that Jesus was good and did all these things in order to please God. Let the child see how fine it is to be 'one of God's friends' and how much it pleases God when we say 'yes' at once and are good 'like Lord Jesus was'.

2. JESUS AT NAZARETH WITH ST JOSEPH (Luke 2 : 29-30, 51-52)

At Nazareth, our Lord Jesus often went into the room where Joseph was working, to help him and work with him.

He watched him without making any noise, and when Joseph needed some tool, like a hammer, or a saw, or a piece of wood, Jesus would give it to him. When Joseph explained to him how the work had to be done, Jesus listened to him and then tried to do it too.

St Joseph, seeing how well Jesus worked, how well he listened and how much he tried to help, was very happy and said :

> 'The Lord Jesus is great !
> He does everything well !
> The Lord Jesus is good !
> He helps all men !'

THE GREATNESS AND GOODNESS
OF THE LORD JESUS AMONG MEN

In presenting an incident from the public life of our Lord, our intention should be not to hold him up before the child as a model, but rather to arouse the child's wonder and love for him. Only when the child feels attached to Jesus in a really religious way are we able to suggest, and then only at exactly the right moment and with the greatest restraint, that he should try to be 'like' Jesus. It is perfectly natural that when the child has come to see how good and how great Jesus was he will be drawn towards him and want to think and do as he did.

There is no need at all to introduce the child to every one of the events we deal with here. It is confusing to pass too quickly from one incident to the next, without dwelling on each for a week or two. If, between Christmas and the Passion, there is only time for two or three stories to be dealt with thoroughly, then so much the better. It is probably best to begin with Jesus and the children : this incident is the best bridge between Jesus as a child himself, and his adult life.

1. OUR LORD AND THE CHILDREN (Mark 10 : 13-16)

Our Lord Jesus grew up and became a man.
When he was thirty years old, he left his home in Nazareth

and set out along the road for different cities so that everyone might have the joy of seeing him and hearing him.

Very many people wanted to see Jesus, listen to him and ask him questions. They all crowded around him.

When they heard him talking and when they saw how kind he was to everyone they said :

'What wonderful things he says !
And how good he is !
He is really the Friend of us all !
(*Or* He is really the Son of God !)'

Some children wanted to see Jesus too and tried to get near him, but the grown-up people standing near pushed them away and said, 'Jesus didn't come here to talk to little children !'

But Jesus scolded the grown-ups for saying this : 'Let little children come to me, and don't stand in their way.'

The children were very happy to hear this, and came to Jesus. Mothers brought their little babies too.

Jesus hugged them and blessed them and the children stayed by him, some standing, some sitting and some kneeling. And they were very happy to be able to hear him speak about God, their Father in Heaven, and to stay there with him. They said to themselves :

'Our Lord Jesus is good !
He is a Friend to little children and to everyone !'

Jesus looked at each child and put his hand on each one's head to bless him. How happy these children were to be near Jesus ! And Jesus was happy to have them near him : our Lord loves children very much and loves you too.

After this the children can gradually acquire the habit of praying before a picture of Jesus, speaking to him in their own words, asking, thanking, etc. Later, they can learn that they can pray even where there is no picture, for Jesus can hear us always. They can learn too about the church, which is the House of God.

Something can also be said about priests being the representatives of Jesus on earth. He has sent them to us to teach us in his place, and we must listen to them as we would listen to him.

JESUS' WORDS The children can sometimes imagine they are children of Palestine, listening to Jesus telling them about God, and how to be God's friend. Get them to listen to one of his discourses, e.g. : what he said about the Father in heaven who cares for the flowers in the fields, the birds of the air (Matt 6 : 26, 28, 30) and develop from this the theme of God 'Our Father in heaven', and also the theme of creation.

:what he said about loving God : 'Love the Lord thy God with all thy heart, all thy mind and all thy strength' (Matt 22 : 35-38).

:what he said about loving others : use the words Jesus used to his apostles before he left them 'Love one another as I have loved you' (John 13 : 34-35).

:or tell the story of the grains of wheat or the mustard seed (Matt 13 : 31-32; Mk 4 : 26-28). Explain that a friend of God is like a little grain of wheat, which is put in the ground and then grows and grows and produces much fruit, not like a seed which stays in the ground doing nothing—that will always stay small, and never grow into anything. This can be illustrated by planting some seeds in a pot and watching them grow, and contrasting this with another pot where the seeds have not been watered and therefore do not grow. Such an illustration can effectively make the words of Jesus more real to him and be of great help.

2. THE CALMING OF THE TEMPEST (Mark 4 : 35-41)

The Apostles, the friends of Jesus, were in a boat going across a big lake. Jesus was with them.

All of a sudden, a big storm blew up. The waves became very rough, the rain fell, the thunder roared. The Apostles were very frightened, and said, 'We shall fall into the water and drown!'

But our Lord Jesus was there. The Apostles looked at him and called to him for help.

Jesus stood up and said : 'Why are you afraid? Am I not with you?' And he put out his hand and ordered the wind and

the water to be still. The wind stopped and the waves calmed
down and everything was at peace.

The Apostles said to themselves:

'The Lord Jesus is great and strong!
The wind and the water obey him!
We are not afraid when he is with us!'

Help the children to understand how, in their own lives,
Jesus is with them and they are safe with him.

3. Jesus Cures a Man Who Could Not Walk (Mark 2 : 1-12)

There was a man who had been sick and could not walk,
and no one was able to cure him. He was very sad.

One day, some friends carried him to our Lord Jesus who
was in a house. The sick man saw Jesus near him and he was
filled with happiness and said to himself : 'Jesus will make me
well again.'

Jesus put his hand out to the sick man and said : 'Stand up,
pick up your bed and walk home.' The man stood up and did
as Jesus told him. He was well again!

The people who were standing around were filled with
wonder at what Jesus had done and praised him saying :

'Our Lord Jesus is great and good!'

And the man who had been sick thanked him and praised
him too.

This story provides a good opportunity to draw the child's
attention to his own healthy limbs and to thank God for them,
to pray for the sick, and to think of ways of being helpful to
those who are sick, weak or old.

4. The Good Samaritan (Luke 10 : 30-37)

This is a story which one day our Lord Jesus told the
people who were listening to him :

A man, travelling along a road, met some robbers. They beat
him and took his things away, and they left him bleeding and

badly hurt, lying by the roadside. He was so badly hurt that he could not walk any farther.

Someone passed by and saw him, but he went on without taking any notice of him. Someone else came by, but he too went on without helping.

Then a third man, from a different country called Samaria, came by, riding on an ass. He saw the wounded man, got down from his ass and lifting up the poor man, did what he could to make his wounds better, and took him farther on to an inn (a warm house where he could lie in a warm bed and be looked after). The man from Samaria left money with the inn-keeper so that he would look after the wounded man well and went on with his journey.

And Jesus asked : 'Who was most kind to the wounded man, the first man who passed by, the second, or the man from Samaria?'

Yes, it was the Samaritan.

Then Jesus added to those who were listening : 'You have to be kind and helpful like the good Samaritan too. You should learn to love one another as I have loved you.'

This can be acted out, and used as the basis for discussing with the children how to be God's friend and how to comfort those who are in need. Show them how the Samaritan acted, the same way as Jesus did when he healed the lame, etc.

LENT There is no question at this age of asking the child to make sacrifices or great efforts during Lent in preparation for Easter. Two or three weeks before Easter he could be told, however, to try to do everything especially well to prepare for the great feast of Easter. It is a good opportunity to help a child to overcome some fault or improve his behaviour in some way, but to do it in a joyful and positive way, imitating Jesus by doing things well.[1]

---

[1] (See above pp. 102-7).

THE GREATNESS AND GOODNESS OF
THE LORD JESUS ON THE CROSS[1]

1. JESUS TELLS THE APOSTLES THAT HE WILL DIE AND RISE AGAIN (Matt 16 : 21-22; 17 : 22-23; 20 : 17-19; John 10 : 10-17; 11 : 50-52; 12 : 23-24 . . .)

One day when Jesus was with his friends, the twelve Apostles, he said to them :

'Soon we shall go to Jerusalem, the great city, and there some people are going to take me, nail me to a Cross and kill me. But three days later, I will come alive again, I will rise again.'

Jesus' friends were sad because they didn't want him to die on the Cross. 'Lord,' they said, 'Do not let yourself be taken by those people and put on the Cross to die.'

'Yes,' Jesus answered, 'I am going to let the people take me and put me on the Cross and die *for you* because I love you. But do not be sad : three days later I will rise again and be alive.'

But his friends were still sad and did not want him to die on the Cross, and they begged him not to go.

'Yes,' Jesus answered, 'I must go. If I do not die on the Cross, and if I do not rise up again you will never be able to become good enough to be God's friends. But if I go, then when I come alive again I will help you forever to become God's friends. Do not be sad.'

It is true, children, Jesus had to go to Jerusalem and let himself be killed on the Cross for us, and rise again three days later. He wanted to do it because he loved us very much and wanted to make us into God's friends.

Then turn with the child towards the crucifix on the wall, and say a prayer something like this one (with hands together) :

> Lord Jesus wanted to go on the Cross,
> He wanted to die on the Cross,
> And rise on Easter Day,
> Because he loves us so much,
> And wants us to grow very good.
> Thank you, Lord, for what you have done for me.

[1] On how to present this, see above, p. 105-6.

This account of the mystery of the Cross should be gone over several times before passing on to the incident of the Palms. Lay stress on the idea that Jesus willed to die so that we might grow good, and be 'friends of God'.

2. JESUS' TRIUMPHANT ENTRY INTO JERUSALEM (John 12: 12-19; Matt 21: 8-16)

Jesus said to his friends : 'Soon we are going to go to the city of Jerusalem; that is where I must die on the Cross for your sakes, and rise again from the dead !'

One day, Jesus said to them : 'Today is the day we must go to Jerusalem. Let us go.' And, with his friends, Jesus set off for Jerusalem.

Jerusalem was the biggest city in the whole country. Many of the people who lived there loved the Lord Jesus. But there were enemies of his. Jesus' enemies said to each other : 'When the Lord Jesus comes into Jerusalem, we will seize him and put him on the cross.' But his friends said : 'When the Lord Jesus comes into Jerusalem, we will hold a great festival in his honour.'

Suddenly, someone shouted : 'The Lord Jesus is coming!'

Straightaway, his friends in Jerusalem prepared a great festival for him : they covered the road along which he would travel with cloaks of many different colours, so that they made a carpet; they cut down branches from the trees so that they could wave them, and they ran out to meet Jesus. The Lord Jesus was riding on a small donkey. When his friends saw him, they held their branches up high, and waved them, and cried out with joy :

'Hosannah !
Long live the Lord Jesus who is coming to visit us !

Long live Jesus, our Saviour !
Long live our king, Jesus !
Hosannah in the highest heavens !'

They all ran along by Jesus' side, shouting out 'Hosannah !' Long live Jesus the Lord ! There were many children among his friends, and they cried out, too : 'Hosannah ! Long live Jesus the Lord !'

But Jesus' enemies were enraged when they heard every-
body shouting 'Long live king Jesus ! They said to the children :
'Be quiet.' But the children went on shouting, louder than ever,
'Hosannah ! Long live king Jesus !'

PROCESSION   This scene can be acted out by the child, who
WITH PALMS   can copy the shouts of the people and their
               waving of branches, etc. A class full of child-
ren can make a palm procession, adding various other shouts
of acclamation and songs of praise for Jesus, who wanted to
die and rise again for our sakes.

3. THE LORD JESUS ON THE CROSS (Matt 26 and Psalm 27)

The Lord Jesus said to his friends : 'They will come and take
me, and hang me on a Cross.'

One day, his enemies came and took him prisoner; they beat
him and nailed him to a cross to kill him. (*Lift up the crucifix
and go on with the story while the child looks at it.*)

Jesus let himself be taken prisoner for our sakes, he let himself be beaten for our sakes, he let them hang him on the cross
because he loved us so much. They took his hands and his feet
and nailed them to the cross. It hurt Jesus very much, but he
did not say a word; he did not cry; he was very brave on the
cross, for our sakes. In his heart, Jesus was saying : 'I will suffer
and die on the Cross for all my friends, for all men on earth,
so that they will be able to be good and be God's friends. In
three days, I will rise again from the dead, I will come back to
life and live for ever and ever, and then all my friends upon
earth will be filled with gladness.'

As this story is repeated during the week, lay stress now on
Jesus' bravery, now on his obedience or his goodness : point
out how he did not hit back, did not lose his temper, how he
actually prayed to his Father not to punish those who were
harming him. Suggest, gently, various ways in which the child
might follow his example.

Say each day, standing in front of the crucifix, with hands
joined, a prayer such as this :

'Lord Jesus you loved us so much when you were on the Cross,
You suffered for us,
And died for us,
So that we should be good, and grow into the friends of God.
Thank you, Lord Jesus.'

Above all, insist on Jesus' love for all men. Perhaps, with great care, tell the child about the great misfortune from which Jesus saved us, in terms of not being God's friend, being wicked in our hearts (do not talk about Hell). Talk about the tremendous joy he wants to give to each individual child. Jesus on the cross is saying to them : I am doing this for you Peter, John, Anne, Elizabeth ... (mention the name of every single child who is listening).

THE SIGN OF THE CROSS   Standing in front of the crucifix, show the child how to make the sign of the cross of Jesus (without saying anything while doing so). This is one way of saying : 'I have not forgotten what you did for me on your cross, Lord. I am your friend. I love you.'

PROCESSION AND ADORATION OF THE CROSS   In the schoolroom, teachers may like to have a procession in honour of the cross (without candles), while the children chant :

'On the Cross, the Lord Jesus loved us !
On the Cross, the Lord Jesus was full of courage !
On the Cross, the Lord Jesus was obedient to his Father !
On the Cross, the Lord Jesus showed his great goodness ! etc.'

Do not leave the child with the idea of the death of Jesus without letting him see its sequel in the Resurrection; suggest, already, the great joy of Easter, which too frequently only means eggs, new toys and holidays to children today.

THE FEAST OF EASTER

It is very important that children should not approach Easter solely with the idea of Jesus dead upon the Cross; they must already see the Cross in the perspective of the Resurrection, and feel a little of the joy of Christ risen from the dead. It is particularly necessary if the children are at school, and breaking up for Easter holidays, to introduce this idea, and prepare them for the joy which is coming. We can tell them : 'Children, it is holiday time. You are having holidays because soon it will be the great feast of Easter. On Easter day, a great candle will be lit in the Church, bells will ring, everyone will be full of joy. Easter is the feast of Jesus risen from the dead and come back to life forever.'

Get the children to say after you, 'Easter is the feast of Jesus risen from the dead and come back to life forever!'

Tell the children to ask their mothers to light a candle during prayers all through Easter week.

Parents can bring their child to feel the joy of Easter by linking it with the joy of the rebirth of nature at Springtime; and, above all, by their own joyful bearing, their smile, patience and good humour. Then, the child will learn that Easter is a Feast when everything and everyone is replenished and made new. Tell the child to be happy and make the rest of the family happy in honour of the risen Lord.

3 THE THIRD STAGE: AFTER EASTER

THROUGHOUT THIS stage, try to find a way to let the child feel joy in the resurrection of Jesus, then real and active love for the Lord who has ascended into heaven. Link this with joy in creation.

When the child hears how at Easter the Lord Jesus rose from the dead, marvellously alive, and came back to his friends, then he will feel the joy and wonder of this event for himself. The signs of spring in the world around him can link this Easter joy with the love that God the creator has for us.

The Ascension will help the child sense the grandeur of Jesus, and at the same time enlarge his idea of heaven.

When, at Pentecost, the child learns how the Lord Jesus sent help to his friends on earth, he will turn to him with joy, courage, goodness, and especially a trusting friendliness. The discovery of the presence of Jesus in the tabernacle will nourish this friendship.

Take care that during the holidays, while the child is perhaps away from school, he does not lose his sense of the presence of God and of the friendship of Jesus which he has come to feel during the year.

During this phase of the programme, add to the pictures of Jesus as an infant in the Crib and Jesus on the Cross, a picture of the Lord risen from the dead. This will help the child form

a more complete idea of the person of Jesus, and of his present
state.

1. AN ANGEL TELLS THE THREE HOLY WOMEN THAT
JESUS IS RISEN (Mark 26 : 1-6; Matt. 27 : 1-8)

The display of a picture of an angel, shining white, seated
on a stone near the open tomb, can give this incident a vivid
impact. Begin the story standing beside the crucifix or a picture
of the tomb; finish the telling with vigour and liveliness.

When the Lord Jesus was dead, his friends took him down
from the Cross and laid his body in a tomb, which was like a
room hollowed out of rock. Then they rolled a huge stone in
front of the mouth of the tomb and went away.

For three days, the body of the Lord Jesus lay there, in the
tomb, behind the great stone.

But on the third day, which was Easter Sunday, an extraordinary thing happened. (*Here, make the child sit down*).

On the morning of this third day, Easter Sunday, three
women who were very good friends of the Lord Jesus, said to
each other : 'We must go to the tomb of Lord Jesus and see
his body, and put sweet perfumes and spices on it.' So they set
off for the tomb. On the way they said to each other : 'Who
can we get to roll away that huge stone ?'

When they came to the tomb, they found that the stone had
been pushed away, and the tomb was open. They went up to
it and looked in: there they saw that the tomb was empty,
Jesus' body was not there any longer. But an angel was there,
sitting on the huge stone, dressed in a white garment, shining
and radiant.

When they saw this angel, the women were frightened and
hid their faces in their hands. The angel said to them : 'Do not
be afraid. You have come to look for Jesus. He is not here.
He has risen from the dead. He is alive !'

Then the three women stood up, very happy, and ran back
to the other friends of Jesus and cried out :

'Allelulia! (*flinging the arms to heaven*)
Be joyful!
The Lord Jesus is risen from the dead!
He will live forever!
Allelulia!

And they were right, children. Jesus had risen from the dead; he came back to life three days after his death. How full of joy his friends were. Now, we will light a candle for Jesus, risen from the dead, and let us all sing: 'Allelulia! Be joyful!'

Then light a candle, set it solemnly in the usual place for prayer, and say with the children the prayer of the holy women. Repeat this prayer every day, in front of the 'Easter candle'. Perhaps also each day have a small procession round the room, carrying the Easter candle, and singing for joy in the resurrection. Take care to associate the candle with the crucifix, so that the child will automatically associate the crucifix not only with the death, but also with the resurrection of Christ.

Do not bring in the idea of the joy of spring until the idea of the joy of the resurrection has been well established in the child's mind. But when this has been achieved, then the child can bring in flowers in honour of the risen Lord.

2. THE LORD JESUS, RISEN FROM THE DEAD, SHOWS HIM-SELF TO MARY MAGDALEN (John 20: 1, 11-18)

There was one woman who loved Jesus very much and did not know that he had risen from the dead. Her name was Mary Magdalen.

Mary Magdalen also went to the tomb on the morning of Easter Sunday to see the body of the Lord. But she did not find his body, since the tomb was empty. Mary Magdalen began to cry, saying: 'They have taken away my Lord and I do not know where he is!'

Suddenly she heard someone behind her. (*Pause here*). It was Jesus, risen from the dead, who was standing there behind her. She turned round. But she did not recognize him. She was crying so much that her eyes were full of tears and she could not see that it was the Lord Jesus standing there. She thought it was the gardener. She said to him : 'Sir, they have taken away my Lord and I do not know where he is. Are you the one who took him away? Tell me where you have put him !'

Then Jesus said to her : 'Mary !' She recognized his voice at once, and then she saw that it was he. There was the Lord Jesus standing next to her, alive. Mary Magdalen was filled with joy and she threw herself down at his feet and said : 'Master !' (*pronounce this word with love and awe*). The Lord said to her : 'Do not touch me. But go and tell my friends that you have seen me !'

Mary Magdalen stood up and ran off to tell Jesus' friends :
'I have seen the Lord.
Allelulia ! Be joyful !
The Lord Jesus has come back to life.
He will live forever.
Allelulia !'

From then on, Mary Magdalen did not cry; she was always filled with joy, because the Lord Jesus was alive, come back from the dead to live forever, and she had seen him.

After telling this story, talk during the week about the joy that comes from having Jesus as your friend at Easter. Discuss with the child ways of sharing this joy with those around you.

THE JOY OF SPRING, AND THE WONDER OF CREATION

To see the rebirth of nature—the budding of the trees, the growth of flowers, to hear bird song again—is to feel in the life of nature the reflected joy of Easter : everything seems to be rejoicing in the resurrection of the Lord. This is a particularly good time of the year to bring the child to see the greatness and goodness of God in the work of creation. Now the child has a chance to come into a more constant and natural contact with the invisible God of heaven, to learn from what he sees around him about his Father in heaven's friendship and care for him. To this end, begin to thank 'God' rather than Jesus, and to address to him the various prayers about creation which you make with the child.

THE GREATNESS AND GOODNESS OF GOD IN CREATION   We have hitherto insisted that the child should be brought to know God from incidents drawn from Scripture; this discovery of God through the Bible, within the framework of the liturgical year, is of the utmost importance; from it the child will gain a truer, more religious, more genuine sense of God, one which will nourish and sustain his whole future religious development. Only after this groundwork has been laid, and the child has come to know the mysterious greatness and fatherly care of God from the Bible should he be brought to draw the same idea from the facts of nature which surround him.

Then the revelation from the Bible must be underlined by contact with God the Creator through the wonders of nature. From this contact the child will be able to establish a link between whatever he sees that is beautiful, whatever gives him joy, and God who is the living source of all things.

Start with the creation of the actual things which the child can see. Use the expression 'God made' very sparingly, lest the child should associate God with the human idea of making; say, rather, 'God gives us' these things, he 'put' them there for us, 'makes them grow', 'gives them their lovely colours'.

FROM LOOKING AT A FLOWER TO PRAISE OF THE CREATOR   For example, start with the detailed observation of one particular thing : let us say it is a flower which the child has picked. As you look at it closely together, noticing the way in which it is made, bring out in the child the joy and wonder that the sight of this flower can arouse. The more directly you can convey to the child the beauty of the flower, the more easily the child will be able to discover, through it, the greatness and goodness of the Creator.

Then, still looking at the flower, say something along these lines :

'How great God is !
He made this lovely flower.'

6

'How good God is !
He made this lovely flower for us.
He put all the flowers in the world there for us.'

It follows quite naturally from that to bring the child to
praise God and thank him :

'Thank you Lord, for this lovely flower.
Thank you for all the flowers you have put in the world !'

'Lord, how great you are ! You have given us . . .'
'Lord, how good you are ! You have given us . . .'

'Lord, we bless you for all the lovely flowers you have made
grow on this earth, for the daffodils, the roses etc. etc. (naming
all the flowers the child knows by name).'

During the week, to follow this lesson, give each child a
flower to hold; get them to examine it carefully, then to pray
to God, lifting the flower up to heaven. Accustom the child
to use this gesture of holding up to God, in a prayer of praise
and thanksgiving, those beautiful things which he has received
from God—a gesture which imitates Simeon's raising up to
heaven the child Jesus in the Temple; and which is a preparation for the priest's gesture of offering at Mass.

Try to go for a walk together in a park, or on an open stretch
of ground, or to the zoo; share the child's enthusiasm and
wonder for everything he sees there. Later, get him to draw
whatever he likes about what he has seen, and offer these drawings to God in thanksgiving.

The child should have every opportunity of coming into
contact with the wealth of creation : sunlight, water, fire,
leaves, birds, butterflies : show him in everything he sees the
bounty and the fertility of the gift of life which exists every-
where, in everything around him, and in the fact of his own
birth too. God is calling the child to give himself to others, to
share what he has himself received. Whenever the child is en-
thusiastic, filled with wonder over something he has seen or

found, lead him to the thought of God. Let him see that everything that gives him pleasure and joy comes from God and
has its life from God: his parents and family, as much as
things in nature; his friends; his own body, whose strength and
skill he is so proud of. God gave him the legs that run so fast,
the arms that are so strong. God wants there to be children,
who will one day grow up and do grown-up things; he wants
them one day to have children of their own, and that is why he
has made both boys and girls.

But the best thing God ever gave us was the Lord Jesus,
and especially Jesus risen from the dead, whom we will meet in
heaven, full of light and life.

> Thank you, Lord, for the flowers which grow,
> > For the sunshine,
> > the song of birds,
> > the animals in the fields,
> > and the babies in our homes.
>
> Thank you most of all for the Lord Jesus,
> > who came down to us,
> > and rose again from the dead.
> > He is in heaven now,
> > And we will see him one day,
> > With the angels and the saints.
> > > Allelulia.

DURING MAY   Another wonderful gift from God was the
Virgin Mary, 'full of grace', more beautiful
than all the flowers on earth.

During May, have a picture of Mary in the room; let the
children bring flowers each day to set before it; say each day the
angelic salutation. In this way, the child will come to associate
Mary with the resurrection of Christ.

After Ascension, talk about the presence of Mary in heaven
close to the Lord Jesus. From heaven she hears the child's
prayer, and can help him. But do not make a habit of calling
her 'your mother in heaven'; refer to her as the mother of the
Lord Jesus.

To the first part of the 'Hail Mary' can now be added the words 'Holy Mary, mother of God, pray for us'. And also, as a prayer, comment on each part of the 'Hail Mary' : on the first part, as a sort of litany of praises drawn from the beauties of creation and from the liturgy : 'You are more beautiful than the sun, etc.'; on the second part, as a litany of petition : 'Pray for my parents, for my friends, for all the children in the world, etc.'

JESUS, IN THE GLORY OF HEAVEN, IS THE CHILD'S FRIEND

1. THE ENTRY OF THE LORD JESUS INTO THE GLORY OF HEAVEN (Luke 24 : 50-52; Acts 1 : 8-10; Matt. 28 : 20b; John 14 : 3, 18-19; Apoc. 5 : 1-4)

This is how the Lord Jesus entered into the glory of heaven.

After the Lord rose again from the dead, he didn't stay with his friends for ever. He stayed with them for only forty days.

After forty days, he said to them : 'Come with me to the top of the mountain.' And he set off with them for the mountain. When they came to the top of the mountain, he said to them: 'Now I am leaving you, and going to heaven, to God my Father (*arms outstretched, looking up towards heaven*). When I am in heaven, I will not forget you : I will help you. And, one day, I am going to bring you to heaven to be with me for ever.'

Then the Lord Jesus went into the great light of heaven, to God his Father. His face was shining like the sun, his clothes were white and full of light.[1]

The angels in heaven sang for joy :

'Glory be to Jesus in heaven. Amen. Allelulia.'

When they saw him go towards heaven, his friends on earth said to each other : 'The Lord Jesus has gone to heaven, gone to God his Father. One day we too will go to heaven, to be with the Lord Jesus, for ever and ever. Allelulia !'

Jesus really did go to heaven to be with God his Father. Great was the joy of the angels and of his friends on earth. It

---

[1] These descriptive details are taken from the description of the transfiguration, when Our Lord surely wanted to show, in advance, what his glory would be like. The angel's prayer is inspired by Apoc. 5, 7, 19.

is a great joy for us, also, because Jesus is now in heaven and one day we will go to him and stay with him for ever.

Now we will light the Easter candle and say the prayer the angels said : 'Glory be to Jesus. . . .'

In silence, and solemnly, light the candle, raise it and say the angel's prayer. Finish with a deep bow.

THE GLORY During the week return to the subject of the
OF JESUS glory of Jesus in heaven, where he is full of light and joy and where the angels bow down to him and sing to him :

> 'Glory be to Jesus in heaven.
> Glory be to Jesus, king of kings.
> Praise the Lord Jesus . . . Alfelulia !'

HEAVEN Come back to Jesus' words : 'I will make a place
AND HELL ready for you' in order to develop in the child the hope of heaven. But do not talk about Hell. If he brings the subject up himself, say : 'Hell is not an interesting place, for God is not there, Jesus is not there. Heaven is where they are.' If he has heard frightening tales of Hell and seems to be worried about it, reassure him : 'Hell is not a place for God's friends. We are God's friends, and Jesus wants all his friends to be with him in heaven.'

THE FRIENDSHIP Do no talk about heaven too much, do not
OF JESUS turn the child's mind exclusively towards heaven. The child must find God in this world, he needs to live with the friendship of the Lord Jesus, and that is what we want to bring out in the stories which follow. Remind him that the apostles, when they saw him going up into heaven, thought of his words : 'I will not forget you.' And Jesus watched over them from heaven and helped them with what they had to do.

2. JESUS, IN HEAVEN, GIVES STRENGTH AND COURAGE TO
    HIS FRIENDS (Matt. 18 : 20; John 14 : 16-19; Acts
    1 : 8; 11 : 1-4, 32-33, 38)

Next Sunday is the feast of Pentecost (*pronounce the word
very distinctly*).

On the day of Pentecost, a most remarkable thing took place.
Listen carefully, and I will tell you what happened. (*Get the
children to sit down*).

The Lord Jesus, before he went up into heaven, had said to
his apostles : 'When I am in heaven, I will not forget you, I will
send the Holy Spirit to you to give you strength and courage,
and he will change your hearts completely.'

Jesus' friends waited in a house for Jesus to send the Holy
Spirit, who was going to bring them such strength and courage.
On the day of Pentecost, Jesus in heaven said : 'Today is the
day I am going to give the Holy Spirit to my friends.'

At that very moment, Jesus' friends heard a great wind from
heaven which filled the whole house they were waiting in, and
they saw fire coming down from heaven. The fire turned into
little tongues of flame which came onto the head of each of
Jesus' friends. Before, they had been very frightened that they
would be caught by Jesus' enemies and put into prison; but
now, they were afraid of nothing, because Jesus had sent them
his Holy Spirit to make them brave. Before, they had not dared
even talk to anyone; now they talked to everyone they met, and
told them, 'The Lord Jesus is in heaven. He has sent us his
Holy Spirit. You must become Jesus' friends also, and then he
will send you also his Holy Spirit.'

Finish this story with a prayer like this :

> 'Lord, give us your Holy Spirit,
> So that we may be very strong,
> And very brave,
> Like the apostles.'

From this story the children will retain the idea of strength
and courage coming from Jesus in heaven, rather than any
clear notion of the Holy Spirit. But, with frequent repetition
of the story, they will gradually come to link the name of this
divine person with the dynamic effects of his presence. This

will be their first intuition, however partial, of the Holy Spirit; and it will grow richer and more real to them as the child's interior life develops.

3. ONE OF JESUS' ENEMIES BECOMES HIS FRIEND (Acts 9 : 1-19; 22 : 10)

There was a man who did not like the Lord Jesus at all and who did a great deal of harm to his friends. This man's name was Saul.

One day Saul was riding his horse, with some soldiers, along a high road. He was on his way to hunt down some of Jesus' friends. Suddenly a great light appeared in the sky (*make a gesture of recoil*). So bright was the light that Saul became blind and fell off his horse onto the ground.

And then, out of the light, came the voice of the Lord Jesus, who said to him : 'Saul, Saul, why are you hurting me.'

Saul said : 'Who are you Lord?'

'I am Jesus, and you are hurting me.'

Then Saul asked : 'Lord, what do you want me to do?'

'Get up,' said the Lord, 'and go into the town of Damascus which lies in front of you. There one of my friends will tell you what you must do.'

Saul got up. The soldiers took him by the arm and led him into Damascus, and there one of Jesus's friends said to him : 'Saul, the Lord Jesus has chosen you to be his friend.' And the man put his hands on Saul's head.

At that moment, Saul's eyes were opened, and he was like a new man: he became a very great and good friend of Jesus. Before, he had done wicked things, now he did good, and was kind to everyone. He had become a 'friend of God'.

From that day, Saul changed his name; his new name was Paul, Saint Paul.

Try, during the week in which this story is recapitulated, to bring home the point of the story to the child : to hurt and make unhappy his parents, his brothers and sisters, his friends (who are Jesus' friends too), is to hurt Jesus and make Jesus unhappy; to be kind to them and make them happy is to make Jesus happy too.

There are various things the child can do to help him come closer to Jesus : imitate Paul's obedience to Jesus : 'Lord, what do you want me to do?'; imitate Paul's obedience to Jesus' friend : for the child this means mother, father, teacher, priest; talk to the Lord Jesus in prayer, desire to see him in heaven, etc.

THE GREATNESS AND GOODNESS OF THE LORD JESUS IN THE TABERNACLE

We have dealt with the life of Jesus upon earth, and of his life in heaven after his ascension. His presence in the Tabernacle should not be ignored, particularly when dealing with children who have a Christian background at home. Many parents and teachers will not have waited until now to take their children to the Church. They may also already have had occasion to talk to them about the presence of Jesus in the Host. We have already suggested a visit to the 'House of the Lord' in the first phase of this programme (see above p. 136). But on that occasion we did not suggest discussing the presence of Jesus in the Tabernacle.

How the child will react to the presence of Jesus in the Church will depend on the sort of image of Jesus we have already conveyed to him, and especially, at this time of the year, on what sort of picture he has in his mind of Jesus risen from the dead and ascended into heaven. The presence in the tabernacle should carry some of the same grandeur, at once mysterious and friendly, as Jesus in heaven. The altar and Tabernacle should seem to the child to be a sacred place, where he can come into contact with the Lord in a very religious and intimate way.[1]

---

[1] We are aware that there is a trend in current educational opinion which would keep back until as late as possible the revelation of this presence in the tabernacle. Father K. Tilmann, who has considerable authority in these matters, says that the child should first of all be told about the Mass, and that the presence of Jesus in the Tabernacle should be talked about only after a long and gradual initiation to the 'meal of the children of God'; this implies that the child will not learn of the presence in the Tabernacle

Our Lord and Friend wants us to meet him there, in a way which is most immediate to our senses and most efficacious, before we are able to meet him in heaven. This meeting is fully consummated in the Mass and Communion, but it is made already possible in some way by coming into the Presence of the Tabernacle with faith and love. This contact, which answers so many of the needs of the child's nature, so many of the desires which grace arouses in him, should be a foretaste of his communion.

1. THE VISIT TO THE TABERNACLE

PREPARATION   Prepare for the visit to the Church carefully without talking about the Tabernacle. For example, say to the child: 'We are soon going to visit Lord Jesus in the Church, which is his house. When Mary Magdalen saw Jesus after he had risen from the dead, she threw herself down on the ground at his feet. When the angels stand before Jesus in heaven they behave with great respect and bow down to him. In the Church we are going to try to be like Mary Magdalen and the angels. We will go in silently, we will walk slowly up to the Lord's table; when we are in front of his table we will bow down to Lord Jesus and keep quite still. . . . We must make our bodies behave properly, and bow down properly to the Lord.'

Now show the child how to walk, how to bow, etc. For the first few visits, it is better not to genuflect, which is too complicated a movement for a little child.

until he is very near the age of reason (*Fiches Vérité et Raison*, no. 242). It seems to us a very serious matter not to sow in the hearts and minds of children from a Christian background, before the age of reason, and even at a very young age, some sense of the actual presence of the Lord in the Tabernacles of churches. The initiation of a young child who is baptized and comes from a Christian family much more able to grasp the quality of presence and of love in the Eucharist than he is to understand the quality of offering to God and of the meal of the Lord: this is a very different thing from the initiation of an adult catechumen, with whom it is right to proceed from the discussion of the Mass to that of the reservation of the Blessed Sacrament.

*

THE VISIT When the child is prepared, make the visit, keeping silence from the time you enter the Church door, and doing nothing more than the movements mentioned above. Walk right up to the altar rails, bow deeply, eyes lowered. Then leave in silence, with the same respect and the same calm demeanour as you entered.

If the child is fidgeting, then after a moment's silence point to the Tabernacle and say : 'The Lord Jesus is there, let us bow down to him.'

In this way the presence of Jesus will be associated first of all with the whole feeling of the church, then with the idea of the altar, with the Tabernacle covered with the canopy, the crucifix and the sanctuary lamp : these are all indirect signs of the presence of the Eucharist, which the Church in her wisdom has thought good to make use of. It is surely wise to let the child absorb these signs of faith, and through them to gain an idea, not too literal or limited, but surrounded with an aura of grandeur, spirituality and mystery. At another visit, mention to the child that the crucifix is set on the altar to remind us that this is not just any table, but the 'Table of the Lord', so that he does not confuse the Eucharistic presence with the presence of the crucifix.

This way of introducing the child to Jesus in the Tabernacle is very simple, but will certainly convey more of the idea of grandeur to the child than any number of explanations. Should he say to you afterwards, 'I did not see Jesus', say to him 'Neither did I.' But go on to say, with joy, 'But he did see us. The sanctuary lamp was burning, the Tabernacle was covered with its curtain, and that means that the Lord was there.'

Gradually, the word 'Tabernacle' will in this way become familiar, and later one can also introduce the words 'Jesus in the Host', and 'the Host at Mass'. Do not make these realities too explicit, do not limit the presence of Jesus too exclusively to the Tabernacle. The Tabernacle should be invested with mystery and grandeur, and not referred to as 'the little house', where Jesus is waiting behind the 'little door'. The Tabernacle should be referred to as 'The place where Jesus is in the Church'; and, a little later, as 'the place where the Host is kept after Mass'. It is best to begin by emphasizing the mystery and the grandeur of the Tabernacle; but go on to mention its friendliness, its intimacy. After he has bowed low, and in silence, the child can learn to talk naturally to the Lord Jesus, his friend in Heaven, who is here, so close to him, in the Tabernacle.

QUESTIONS THE   If the child asks you to explain how this
CHILD MAY ASK   can be the Lord Jesus, simply affirm your
faith to him : 'The Host looks like a white circle, but it is the Lord Jesus, it is Jesus in the Host. When we see the Host we are full of joy, because this is the Lord Jesus, and we bow down to him. One day, when you are older, you will be able to receive the Lord Jesus, and this will be a great joy to you.'

Certain more advanced children will not be satisfied with this very simple explanation, and will ask for more; tell them, speaking with the great respect which should accompany a matter of such importance, that the Lord, in his love for us, 'wanted to leave us some way we could remember all that he had done for us upon earth, some way we could receive him when we are old enough. That is why he has left us the Host, which is Jesus himself.'

Gradually in this way the idea of the Host will come to be associated for the child with the idea of the Lord Jesus, whom he will one day receive. But remember always to proceed with great prudence. It is always better to say too little than too much.

APPENDIX I

JUSTIFICATION OF THE BIBLICAL APPROACH

THERE ARE many very experienced teachers who are suspicious of this method of bringing little children to a knowledge of God through the use of stories from the Old Testaments. They prefer the discovery of God in creation and in the events in the life of the child. They fear that if the child is saturated with religious revelation from his earliest years he will grow sated and indifferent as the years go on.

It is of course very necessary to proceed with balance and with prudence. But surely such excessive misgivings are the result of the wrong method of biblical presentation? A more thorough acquaintance with the religious resources of early childhood, and our own experience, have led us to different conclusions, particularly in dealing with children from Christian families. Between the ages of three and five the child is very sensitive to grandeur and mystery presented in such a way that it comes home to him. Hence the revelation of God through stories from the Bible fits in exactly with this stage of his psychological development. The child is filled with joy, the deepest needs of his soul are enriched and satisfied when he sees the greatness of God and his fatherly love, his ever-watchful care, his helping presence.

The crux of the problem seems to be not : should we or should we not use biblical stories and religious images in the religious formation of young children, but rather : which stories, which images, should we use to reveal God to the child and to introduce him to the world of supernatural reality? How should we present these? What limits should be observed, what precautions taken?

When one is aware of the deeply felt and long-lasting influence (lasting for a lifetime) of the images, impressions and experiences which are received before the age of reason, how can one leave it until the age of seven or eight to bring the child into contact with the God of the Bible, with some of the great religious figures of the Old Testament, with some of the basic happenings in the life of Christ. Where can the child meet more vividly and really than in the Bible that *living God who speaks to mankind*?

It may be asked whether the Bible was written for children? To which we reply that revelation is for every child of God; each draws from it what he is capable of taking in, and from it draws sustenance for his own spiritual life. The Word of God is not only for adults. It is for us to give it to the child according to his capacity. Our Lord himself has made it very clear that childhood is a time of special ability to enter into the mysteries of the kingdom of God, and experience proves that young children are as well able, and often more able, than adults to understand certain of the essential aspects of the Bible.

At this age there is no question of giving the child a connected course in sacred history, nor of telling him a great many stories at random, nor of telling him any story whatsoever out of the Bible. Prudence must also be exercised in dealing with such topics as the creation, the fall, the flood, etc. But there are many other events which present no difficulty and there is a way of using these stories from the Bible in such a way as to nourish the faith and religious growth of the child, without asking of him an historic sense. It is very difficult to conceive the religious formation of a Christian child, within the tradition of the Church, which keeps that child away from contact with the living God who speaks and acts in the Bible.

As for the objection that the child will grow sated with things religious : this is not a genuine possibility. In subsequent years the child will long to feel again that inner satisfaction, the feeling of growth, which he had from contact with divine power and goodness in the Bible, to feel again that he is close to the Lord Jesus in the events of the Gospel. The child grows weary and stale not from repetition of the same scene and the same idea, not from growing familiarity with a person, but from the presentation of an idea, a person or an event which has no relation at all to his psychological state. If the presentation is adapted, as the years pass, to the changing psychological state of the child, then his interest will grow and be renewed. And for the majority of children, if this condition is fulfilled, what will be preferred and even demanded is stories already half known, characters already half recognized, events already somewhat familiar. This basic deposit in their minds of a fund of familiar images will be a lifelong treasure from which their religious life can be nourished and renewed.

APPENDIX II

A METHOD USING CREATION AS A
STARTING POINT

ANOTHER WAY of bringing the child to an awareness of God takes as its starting point the admiration of God for all his works of creation, an awareness of God's absolute supremacy over all things created. We have already touched on this method (see above, pp. 110-2, 160-4). But we would like to quote here, with the permission of the author, extracts from the notes of Sister St Ignatius, of the Petites Soeurs de l'Ouvrier, whose work has been among young children in completely dechristianized working class areas of France.

GOD
HIS BEAUTY   HIS POWER

PREPARATORY NOTES, FOR CATECHISTS

Before speaking to the children about God's great love, we must bring them to see his beauty, his greatness, his all-power-fulness; we have to try to develop in them the 'sense of God', the sense of the sacred.

I

One day, I showed a very beautiful rose to a little girl, and she looked at it for a long time; then she said to me : 'There is nothing in the world more beautiful than that.'

One day I saw a tiny baby smiling at its mother, and the mother said to me : 'There is nothing in the world more beautiful than my baby.'

Another day, I was walking with a boy in a pine forest; the pine trees were covered with snow; he looked at them for a long time, and then he said to me : 'Nothing in the world could be better than this.'

I said to the little girl who was looking at the rose : 'No, your rose is not the most beautiful thing in the world; there is something even more beautiful, someone so beautiful that if you could see him, you would be so dazzled you would die, you would not be strong enough to look at someone so very, very beautiful.'

This someone who is so very beautiful is GOD.
What did I say to the little boy?
What did I say to the mother with her baby?
Everything we see on earth, all the beautiful flowers, the beautiful children, all this is nothing compared with the tremendous beauty of God.
The angels in heaven are so happy when they look on the great beauty of God that they say, over and over again :
'Holy, holy, holy, Lord God almighty.'
And children too, and fathers and mothers who know how beautiful the good God is, say like the angels :
'Holy, holy, holy, Lord God almighty.'

II

One day, I was walking by the sea when a great storm blew up and the waves were as high as houses; a sailor said to me : 'There is nothing at all stronger than that storm.'
A man was talking about a rocket, so powerful and strong, and he said : 'No one could be more powerful, no one could be cleverer than the man who invented that rocket.'

I said to the sailor, 'There is someone who is more powerful than the storm, and that is God.'
What did I say to the man?
The angels are so happy to see the beauty and the power of God that they say, standing before God :

'Holy, holy, holy, Lord God almighty.'
And children, too, who know that God is very strong, very beautiful, what do they say?

III

One day, a boy at the High School said to his mother : 'No one could be as clever as my teacher, he knows everything.'
His mother said to him: 'Your teacher is certainly very clever. But there is only one person in the world who knows everything !'
This person is . . . . (make the children say it)
Who is more beautiful than the most beautiful things in the world?
Who is stronger, more powerful than everything in the world?
Who is it who sees everything, knows everything?
When they think of all this, the angels in heaven, children, fathers and mothers, all say together to God :
'Holy, holy, holy, Lord God almighty, heaven and earth are full of the glory of God.'

Sister St Ignatius uses these little conversations in unison with the biblical approach to the sense of God, and makes use of certain of the biblical stories we have given in this book, such as the calling of Abraham and of Moses. Her comments on this approach reinforce what we have already said :
'How are we to arouse in the children this sense of God? Our own awareness of the holiness of God—and we must ask the Holy Spirit to make this sense more active in us—must show in our physical attitudes of respect, in the tone of voice which we use, whether this be grave, mysterious or solemn. The children will sense from our behaviour how great is this God of whom we are talking, even if they cannot understand everything we say. We really have to act out for them, to mime God's gesture in commanding Abraham to leave his country, to make the scene with the burning bush vivid and real through our acting . . . "Do not come near" . . .'
That is how the children will first grow aware that God is

infinitely higher than man. However it is done, the child's first contact with God, especially at school, should invariably be stamped with the same respect and awe that we find in the Bible.